Quest for Reality: Christianity and the Counter Culture

Carl F. H. Henry
and others

InterVarsity Press
Downers Grove, Illinois 60515

Nov 1, '73

InterVarsity Press
is the book publishing
division of Inter-Varsity
Christian Fellowship.

ISBN 0-87784-761-4

Library of Congress Catalog
Card Number: 73-75892

Printed in the United
States of America

Contents

1793430

Introduction by Carl F. H. Henry

VI
Summaries

Introduction

The temper of the university world is today predominantly naturalistic. If dialectical materialism dominates the communist sphere of nations, technocratic scientism inspirits the secular society of the West. Their common hallmark is the comprehension of the external world solely in terms of impersonal relationships and continuities.

The cost to contemporary man of this eclipse of ultimate spiritual and moral realities is more staggering than he imagines. Reduction of the world to natural processes and events carries the price tag of the loss of any absolute truth and of all enduring ethical norms. Everything is considered transient and contingent, and relative to its cultural matrix; man is himself enthroned as lord of the cosmos and of history, the maker of meaning, temple of truth and vehicle of values in an otherwise impersonal universe.

These haughty pretensions are, to be sure, logically incompatible with the naturalistic credo taken seriously; on its premises, man is at best a cosmic tramp destined for oblivion, and his notions of personal importance and social utopia, of shared meaning and worth, have no basis whatever in a universe emerging from an unpredictable explosion and heading toward inevitable decomposition. The options actually facing sensate man are either to maintain his significance and worth on the basis of grandiose myths or to draw the sceptical and nihilistic inferences latent in a philosophy of change and decay.

There is, of course, another alternative, whose long roots go back to New Testament and indeed to Old Testament times: the biblical view of God and man and the world. Far from being obsolete, this view is championed by a competent vanguard of evangelical scholars such as those associated with the Institute for Advanced Christian Studies. IFACS is a mobile fellowship of academicians who find the logic of Christian theism more compelling than recent speculation which has already sagged from humanism to existential atheism. The Christian revelation explains man's lapse from faith, his propensity for myths and his ineradicable ties to the God of creation who would make all things new.

Technocratic scientism has failed to fulfill the utopian hopes of those who have made it an object of trust. Its emptying of the categories of truth, meaning and progress into the impersonal continuities at the heart of scientific empiricism has banished from the externally real world any importance for the personal reality of God and the personal significance of man. Against this scientific reductionism not only have competent theologians and philosophers voiced an incisive protest, but many competent scientists as well. They emphasize that the real supports of truth, meaning and progress lie in the spiritual and moral world, and that God is the indispensable source of security and serenity in life. The technocrats, it may be said, not only are less than theists but often show themselves to be less than empirical scientists, through the dogmatic assertions they volunteer about the nature of the whole of reality.

Some of the most virile movements of our time are now directed against technocratic materialism. The youth counter culture, disenchanted by the scientific outlook on life, has disaffiliated itself and is pursuing a multi-pronged quest for transcendent realities. Academicians too are taking a long and hard look at the metaphysical veto encouraged by logical positivists and still maintained by some analytical philosophers.

Amid this ferment the Institute for Advanced Christian Studies sponsored an invitational scholars' conference to bring into focus frontier trends and issues and to see them in the light of the best of evangelical thought. "Christian Perspective on THE SEARCH FOR REALITY in Modern Life" was held at O'Hare Inn, Chicago, in October of 1971, at a time when the Jesus movement was just emerging as a directive spiritual effort across the nation. What should the attitude of Christians be toward the counter culture and its various manifestations? What is authentic, what is inauthentic and what does Christian mission require in the way of support and response? IFACS welcomes this opportunity to share the content of this conference with a wider company.

May, 1973   *Carl F. H. Henry*

I

The Loss & Discovery of the Personal

Some Clinical Sketches of the Youth Culture
by Armand M. Nicholi II

The mass media have made us aware of the rather recent changes in our society involving numbers of young people turning from a grossly secular style of life to one overtly spiritual. This interest in the spiritual began several years ago, emerging as part of the widespread use of hallucinogenic drugs. At that time it centered primarily on Eastern religions—perhaps because they were not part of the Establishment—but recently it involves the Christian faith, focusing primarily on the person of Christ, expressing itself in small groups and so-called Christian communes. The institutional church has yet to become a major part of the movement.

That the movement has taken place among the young has particular significance, for in our present society youth has been setting the standards. Adults, rather than taking the lead, anxiously attempt to imitate youth. The adult world has adopted their dress, their language, their music, etc. In Boston, which calls itself the cultural hub of the universe, it is almost impossible to find a radio station that plays any music but rock. In the movies, on television, in books, plays and advertisements—in every facet of our culture—one observes the indelible influence of youth. When parents imitate children, when the adult world turns to the adolescent world for its values and standards, problems inevitably arise. The young, struggling to find a clear inner definition of themselves, have a need to be separate from adults. When adults identify with them, adopting their dress and mannerisms, the distance many young people find comfortable and necessary to maintain becomes threatened. Thus they resort to absurd behavior and dress.

What are the determinants of recent interest in Christianity among the young? Will this trend also influence the adult world and perhaps be the beginning of a vast spiritual transformation within our society? This doesn't appear likely at the moment, judging from the rather startling reactions of parents to the conversion of their teenagers, which were recently printed in *Life* magazine. Is the interest merely a passing adolescent fad that will disappear as quickly as their current dress, music and mannerisms? This youth culture changes so rapidly that a college senior is considered by a college freshman to be a different generation. Being five years out of college makes one a different species.

As with all human behavior, this spiritual interest among youth is multi-determined. We could consider it from many perspectives. Sociologists might point to the cultural crisis we have been in for the past few decades and say this phenomenon is but a result of that crisis, that is, a desperate attempt on the part of man to regain the sense of dignity and personal worth he once had when Western civilization was less secular. They might say that our preoccupation with science and technology has destroyed man's image of himself as the center of God's creation and that consequently man has become increasingly restless and discontent. In addition to social and cultural determinants, theologians might point to the many genuine conversions taking place and present good evidence of spiritual forces at work.

I would, however, like to speak from the only perspective from which I am qualified, that of a physician. I would like to share with you some clinical impressions from my work with young people. These impressions may help us understand not only some of the emotional aspects of this youth culture but also, perhaps, some of the psychological determinants of its recent interest in the Christian faith.

DRUGS

One obvious, unique aspect of our present-day culture is its involvement with drugs. I would estimate seventy percent of our population take drugs regularly. These range from marihuana, LSD and heroin, at one end of the scale, to amphetamines, tranquilizers and barbiturates (and we must also include alcohol) at the other. Members of the older generation have long used drugs to alleviate their restlessness, anxiety and discontent: to pick them up, to calm them down, to wake them up, to help them sleep, to stimulate or curb their appetites. With the younger generation, however, drugs are a rather recent phenomenon and one which is now considerably more widespread then most of us realize. About ninety-five percent of the people I see who are under thirty smoke marihuana regularly, and a significant number have taken LSD. During the past couple of weeks, we moved west of Cambridge to Concord, Massachusetts. In one of the high school classes there a teacher asked how many had experienced marihuana, and sixteen of twenty raised their hands. And we know that children of pre-high school age are also being exposed to drugs.

Why this preoccupation with drugs? What does it mean? A short time ago, when the hallucinogenic drugs were getting so much coverage in the news media, I set out to interview about thirty or forty young people who had taken LSD. They were intelligent, well-informed students, who placed a high premium on intellectual activity. I couldn't understand why they would take a drug that obviously jeopardized their intellect and posed a real danger to their mind. I found that each of the drug users was struggling with intense personal conflict, and the promises of what the drug could do in resolving these conflicts far outweighed the risk.

Let me mention briefly some of the common characteristics of these LSD users. First, they described extremely poor relationships with other people. Feelings of loneliness, isolation and estrangement were common themes. The promise of the drug which appealed to this particular conflict was that the drug would make them feel love and at one with others. As Richard Alpert, one of the proponents of the drug, has written, "With LSD you share consciousness and from then on the other person has become a part of you forever and you a part of him in a very meaningful sense."

Another characteristic was an extreme dissatisfaction with self. The users had high expectations for themselves but poor performance. Many had intellectual interests but were unable to settle down sufficiently to become absorbed in these interests. Their dependency and inner conflicts took so much energy there was little to invest in their studies. They found extreme frustration in their desire to engage in creative activities. Here again the drug promised a quick and easy resolution. Proponents of the drug spoke about it in terms of freeing the mind and expanding consciousness.

This group also shared hostility and anger toward the adult world. This anger paralleled a deep-seated dependency, often of infantile proportions. One young lady said, "We take LSD as another way of avoiding the adult world we hate. I think adults want me to fit into a mold and I object. LSD is a way of fighting this mold." The promise of the drug that appealed to this particular attitude was that it would change reality by means of an activity of which the adult world disapproved.

Another characteristic drug users shared were feelings of hopelessness and inadequacy. Many times the drug was taken after an unsuccessful social or sexual encounter. The promise of the drug that appealed to this aspect of their conflicts was that LSD would make them into effective, perceptive and insightful persons. Again and again these young people said they were attracted to the drug because of the promise that it would bring a change in them, a magical change that would straighten out the defects and inadequacies that plagued them.

And one final characteristic was that most of the drug users spoke of a moral and spiritual void in their lives. When they really opened up, they revealed feelings of guilt and moral worthlessness. They spoke of being angry with their parents for not giving them a philosophy of life to fall back on (as their grandparents had given their parents). The drug appealed to this conflict by promising them a mystical experience. They were caught up primarily in Eastern religions. The terms *karma, maya* and *nirvana* became part of their vocabulary.

So much then for the attitudes and conflicts of these young people taking LSD. We can understand how some of these emotional needs—for self-renewal or rebirth, for dealing with guilt, for filling a moral and spiritual void, for establishing a positive image of themselves, for finding a philosophy providing them with some meaning to life—might lead them to drugs that promise to fulfill these needs. But because the drugs inevitably fail, we are seeing today a mass disillusionment with the drug scene and a gradual turning from it to more promising pastures.

POOR IMPULSE CONTROL

In addition to its preoccupation with drugs, our society suffers from a marked inability to control basic impulses. The liberation of sexual and aggressive instincts may be due to many factors. Developments in my field, especially in psychoanalysis, may be partly responsible. Unfortunately, some people felt that freedom from sexual prohibitions would eliminate neurosis and make for a happier society. This, of course, has proved patently untrue. Although Freud felt that excessive suppression of instincts often leads to neurosis and accounts for much restlessness and discontent in our civilization, he also realized the danger of their liberation: "When the mental counter-forces which ordinarily inhibit aggression are out of action, aggression will manifest itself spontaneously and reveal man as a savage beast to whom consideration toward his own kind is something alien. . . . Civilization has to use its utmost efforts in order to set limits to man's aggressive instincts . . . hence the restriction upon sexual life."

A recent article in *The Psychoanalytic Quarterly* has pointed out that drive liberation is the consequence of less pressure on the younger generation by the older generation and that this has not diminished the conflict between generations but has heightened it. It points out that sexual liberation and the easier opportunities for sexual gratification for today's youth have not produced a lessening of aggression. For some reason it seems to have increased restlessness and discontent and conflict between the generations.

One thing we know: Aggression in the form of violence appears to be increasing continuously in our society. Figures released recently by the Attorney General show an eleven percent increase in violent crimes across the country. In Boston there has been a forty-three percent increase in the number of homicides. A murder is committed there about every third day.

I would like to mention some expressions of violence that I have been able to observe clinically in milder form among students. For the past few years demonstrations, riots and strikes have plunged hundreds of college campuses into unprecedented turmoil. I was able to observe first hand one such disorder that occurred a year or two ago and brought the nation's oldest university to an abrupt halt. A small group of students at Harvard seized an administration building and forcibly ejected several of the deans. In quick response the administration summoned outside help. Some of the police that were brought in lost control, and the resulting injuries to both participants and innocent observers radicalized many of the moderates and catapulted the college into a paralyzing strike.

As I explored the details of the crisis, I was struck by the endless examples of disorderly communication occurring especially at high administrative levels and reflecting disordered human relations. One fact emerged with remarkable clarity: The remoteness and invisibility of some administrators had alienated a large segment of the college community and set the emotional backdrop for the disorder.

One of the many emotional responses aroused in students by the distant, inaccessible and unresponsive leaders relates to specific early-life experiences of modern youth and their characteristic emotional profiles. The behavior of remote, uninvolved professors and administrators parallels the behavior of parents in the childhood homes of many of today's students.

An increasing number of young people come from backgrounds in which the family has virtually disintegrated. At no time in history has the integrity of the family been more severely jeopardized by both internal and external forces. A home in which both parents are available to the child, emotionally as well as physically, has become the exception rather than the rule.

Although awareness that absent parents often produce resentful or disturbed children can hardly be considered a recent discovery, we have only recently become aware of the full emotional impact on the child, especially the impact of the inaccessible or absent father. The demands on the time of the father, the changes in the role of the wife and mother, and the intrusion of the television set and other electronic gadgets make meaningful relationships difficult to maintain. The absence and uninvolvement of parents induce in the child repeated feelings of rejection and resentment.

Some current modes of rearing a child also contribute to the difficulty: The failure to set limits intensifies the feeling of unconcern and leaves a residue of poor inner discipline and of inability to delay gratification, and the tendency to punish by withdrawal of attention and affection increases the sense of being unacknowledge and rejected. Among many of the affluent, parents send their children to boarding school, the culmination of a long series of rejections. (It may be more than coincidental that private school students were over-represented among those who forcibly seized Harvard's administration building.)

The particular orientation of modern society, with material values superseding ethical and spiritual values, produces fragmented families, with both parents and children confused as to limits and basic priorities. Perhaps we should not be surprised that many students react against this background by rejecting not only the materialism of our society but the entire free enterprise system as well.

Out of this background come the specific emotional conflicts that trouble young people today. Limitations of space permit only cursory mention of those difficulties that relate to campus turmoil:

1. Depression and excessively low self-esteem. Suspiciousness and hostility toward authority, always present to some degree in this age group, have become considerably more intense and have come considerably closer to the surface. Repressed anger in the child, resulting from a sense of rejection, may in the adolescent express itself clinically in (1) depression (by far the most frequent clinical symptom encountered among students); (2) an excessively negative self-image, exaggerated, as we have discussed, among those taking drugs (the disheveled and unkempt appearance of many young people today not only serves as a conscious gesture of defiance and repudiation of the Establishment but also reflects this unconscious low self-esteem); (3) irrational, stereotyped, destructive behavior.

2. Poor impulse control and an inability to tolerate frustration. Although as recently as ten years ago the majority of clinical problems among college students reflected inhibition and excessive impulse control, emotional difficulties in the young today reflect lack of impulse control (both sexual and aggressive) and inability to tolerate frustration. Perhaps this relates to the expectation of some of the more extreme radicals for immediate response to nonnegotiable demands.

3. Intense sensitivity to unresponsive authority. Most important of all, today's youth possesses a peculiarly intense sensitivity to remote, invisible and unresponsive authority, resulting from early experiences with unresponsive parents in the childhood home.

In addition to campus disorder there is another form of aggression that I would like to mention briefly. I mention it not only because it is a form of aggression turned against the self but because it represents a pervasive symbol of the *Now* generation. I am referring to the motorcycle. The popularity of the motorcycle is something quite recent. In 1956 there were less than a half million registered; in 1971 over five million. The motorcycle is considered by physicians a lethal instrument of destruction. About 5,000 people are killed annually on motorcycles and over a quarter of a million are injured. During the past few years I have observed, quite inadvertently, a group of patients manifesting unusual emotional investment in the motorcycle and sharing a number of general characteristics.

After describing these symptoms as a syndrome (in a paper published in 1970), I received letters from doctors all over the world. The syndrome is widespread. Let me mention briefly its essential features:

1. Unusual preoccupation with the motorcycle. When the patient was not actually riding the motorcycle he daydreamed continuously of doing so.

2. A history of accident proneness extending to early childhood and a recent history of one or more serious motorcycle accidents.

3. Persistent fears of bodily injury.

4. Extreme passivity and inability to compete—academically, athletically or socially.

5. A defective self-image; deep-seated, often unconscious, feelings of being unintelligent, fat, weak, feminine and defective.

6. Poor control of sexual and aggressive impulses, with anger (especially anger toward the father turned inward and resulting in the patient's passivity), depression and a tendency to self-injury.

7. Fear of and counter-phobic involvement with aggressive girls.

8. Impotence and intense homosexual concerns.

9. And finally, what is perhaps most important to our consideration here, a distant, conflict-ridden relationship with the father.

The patient sees the father as excessively critical and as one with whom it is hopeless to compete. Each patient within my sample feared his father and as a young boy had learned to avoid him. The fathers of these patients were highly successful in their careers. Several had the unusual quality of being outstanding as both athletes and scholars, making them, of course, formidable competitors. These busy fathers were emotionally and physically inaccessible to the boys.

FREE SEXUAL EXPRESSION

One other aspect of poor impulse control in our society is the permissive and free expression of sexuality. The type of family background I described earlier results in profound loneliness and a sense of not belonging. A great deal of sexual behavior is an attempt to overcome this loneliness. There appears to be an increasing inability to tolerate being alone. Sexual behavior is often an attempt to find someone to be close to and belong to. Young people seek emotional security through sex, but because their experience is so often disappointing and so often results in emotional pain they become more and more disillusioned. They are not as preoccupied with sex as the older generation and this, of course, is good. They have little interest in X-rated movies. On the other hand, the intensity and pleasure of sexuality has markedly diminished. In this regard Freud made an interesting comment in 1912 when he wrote: "At the same time if sexual freedom is unrestricted from the outset the result is no better. It can easily be shown that the psychical value of erotic needs is reduced as soon as it becomes easy. An obstacle is required in order to heighten the libido. . . . In times in which there were *no* difficulties standing in the way of sexual satisfaction, such as perhaps during the decline of ancient civilizations [and I suppose if Freud were writing today he would include our present civilization as well], love became worthless and life empty."

Another interesting factor is that people today feel a great deal of guilt about their sexual behavior. They don't admit this readily. Here we find another reason for the appeal of the Christian faith. When they speak of the moral and spiritual void in their life, they refer to a gap they feel between their social concerns on the one hand and their personal morality on the other. The Christian faith, of course, with its forgiveness and strong moral precepts, helps bridge the gap.

One final comment about sexuality. I have noticed an increasing incidence of homosexuality among young people. It is difficult to know whether an actual increase exists or whether the freedom to talk about it makes us more aware. The wide coverage afforded homosexuality in the news media, resulting from the recent activity of homosexual organizations and the participation of female homosexuals in the Women's Liberation Movement, has made this a topic that is discussed openly.

As it continues to become more acceptable for discussion, the church will undoubtedly become more aware of this problem among its members. As a matter of fact the church may find a surprisingly large number of its congregation struggling with homosexual impulses. This ought not to be surprising for at least two reasons: (1) The loneliness, the intense need for human contact and the image the homosexual has of himself as a misfit cause him to see the Christian community as a refuge and a possible source of comfort. (2) Recent research findings disclose a statistically significant higher incidence of cold, rejecting fathers within the family background of homosexuals, which produces a yearning for a warm, loving, accepting father. The appeal of Christianity in meeting this particular emotional need is obvious.

What we have looked at are some broad sketches of the youth culture from a clinical perspective. One can't help but raise the question of how representative such sketches are. Current understanding of the human mind reveals that we are much more alike than different. The differences between the conflicts of a person who visits a psychiatrist and one who does not are differences of degree and not of kind. Therefore I believe we have been looking at attitudes and feelings that represent a wide spectrum of youth.

As we focus on these sketches, I think we gain some understanding of the emotional and psychological setting in which interest in Christianity is taking place. We have frequently mentioned poor impulse control. People in my field attribute this to a weakening of the agency they refer to as the super-ego, and psychoanalysts attribute weakening of the super-ego to the tenuous role of the father in the modern home. It is interesting how frequently conflicts with the father and intense ambivalence toward authority occur among the young people we have been discussing. This fact may make Christianity—with its nuclear Father-Son relationship and its provision of a strong, forgiving, accepting Father—emotionally appealing. We have also noticed the strong need to find a means of coping with guilt, to find a moral framework that will give meaning to life, to find some means of loving others and of establishing a positive image of oneself as a human being—all of which may play a part in establishing the psychological determinants of this recent spiritual quest.

I have seen the lives of many students changed from a completely secular life style to a full commitment to Christ. Some who were leaders of the SDS movement that caused the disorder at Harvard were forced to leave college. During their time away they embraced the Christian faith. It's interesting to see how they have changed. Their intense social concerns have by no means diminished, but their methods of expressing these concerns have altered quite radically.

One final point: I would like to see the conversion experiences of these outstanding young people written up and published—not only because the young are more receptive to Christ and his claims than ever before in our lifetime but also because young people are most influenced by what other young people do and think. Peer group pressure, or the lure of the caucus, has always been the most influential force among youth, but today it appears stronger than ever. The most effective witness to them will be the knowledge of what Christ has done and is doing in the lives of other young people.

Selfhood and the Protests of Youth
by James Daane

Armand Nicholi II has given us a perceptive if gloomy analysis of the psychology of that sector of American youth that has become highly visible in the news media and very mystifying to the adult generation. He sees the sudden and extensive recourse to drugs by these young people as an action stemming from their anxieties, and then he considers the way they cope with their hostilities and aggressiveness.

Nicholi sees youth turning to drugs from a base of weakness. Young people feel estranged from others, dissatisfied with themselves, hostile toward their environs, debilitated by a sense of hopelessness and inadequacy, and ridden by a sense of the moral worthlessness of life. The use of drugs provides a temporary escape from their experience of life as a bucket of ashes and, on the other hand, a temporarily heightened sense of euphoria. In between trips they harbor an aggressive sense of hostility that sometimes takes the form of disdain and contempt and sometimes of overt violence against everything outside their own skins. Sometimes their aggression is an expression of contempt for the prevailing culture and takes the form of a counter culture of long hair, shabby clothes, free love and avoidance of the bath. At other times their aggressiveness is a violent effort to destroy the culture in which they live.

In both instances, modern youth feels itself surrounded by a hostile world which threatens its selfhood and its unique worth and reality. As an animal fights instinctively against any odds when its life is at stake, modern youth, feeling that its very self is threatened, abandons the rational and the moral and operates out of mindless instinct. It "does its own thing" and "lets it all hang out," which on the instinctual level means free love, nudity and sexual permissiveness. Such sexual expression is not really sexy. It is, as Nicholi suggests, one way for a threatened self to save itself in an attempt to find community and the assurance of personal worth through another self.

THE SELF AGAINST THE SELF

Yet this free giving of the self to another in sexuality and the recourse to the destruction of all that lies outside one's own skin, whether it be the police, the military, the courts or any other institutionalized form of the Establishment, are in the end self-destructive acts. Youth's hostile aggression against the world ends up in a self-destructive stance in which the self is against the self. No man is an island. The violent destruction of society and its institutions and the permissive violation of another's sexuality are always, and inevitably, self-destructive.

The resulting consequence is, as Nicholi points out, that the young who practice this kind of aggressive hostility, whether in overt violence or covert disdain for all that lies outside their own skins, are increasingly depressed and victimized by an ever-worsening, debilitating and frustrating self-image. The more their destructive aggression is directed against the environment, the more they discover that they are thereby destroying the very reality they sought to preserve.

These protesting young people are looking for something, says Nicholi, more spiritual than their parents sought. They are in protest against a materialistic society; they know better than their parents that man does not live by bread alone. I agree. Their parents fought their way through the thirties. For them the acquisition of bread was an achievement that itself gave meaning to existence. They worked for a living, and their success gave meaning to both their work and their lives. Today few people work for a living, and those that do are too busy to riot in Berkeley or demonstrate in the District of Columbia. People today work for luxuries; they spend their lives for the creature comforts that spell affluence. But the protesting young people of the sixties and seventies see through the hollow meaningless-ness of the Horatio Alger boys and the men in the grey flannel suits. They know that life is more than meat and the body than clothing. They instinctively recognize that the questions "What shall it profit a man if he gain the whole world and lose his soul?" and "What shall a man give in exchange for his life?" are rhetorical questions to which no answers are expected because there are none.

This youth protest is more right than wrong. A society which dedicates its existence to Wall Street, to the mercenary objec-tives of labor unions, to the greater financial profits of giant business corporations at the cost of laying waste the land and despoiling the people, is bent on achieving its own self-destruc-tion. The youth protest knows that the authentic life of the individual and of society does not consist in the abundance of things possessed. In this they are more right than wrong.

Youth faces the question of how it can effectively protest against a Behemoth, a monolithic society whose whole life style and its every representative institution are governed by and dedicated to a form of freedom which is in fact a form of slavery—a soul-withering, dehumanizing and depersonalizing commitment to a credo that material gain and worldly power and glory are of greater value than the human person. How does one deliver effective protest against a materialistic society?

The secular Establishment is formidable, even cunning. The youth protest movement has learned that letting one's hair grow is not enough, for the most ardent exponents of the Establish-ment had cunning enough to absorb this form of protest by adopting the sartorial style of visiting a barber no more than once in three months. Wearing patched blue jeans and the blue shirt of the laboring man of the thirties was not effective, for the Establishment had enough cunning to absorb the new dress style and make money by promoting it. Nor was the youth protest that expressed itself in sexual permissiveness and nudity effective. The Establishment could also absorb this and turn it to profit, as recent movies demonstrate.

The militant "Right On" is now used by people on the right, and the slogan "Power to the People" has been taken up by President Nixon for promoting his revenue sharing plan. When the System absorbs the protests and, without changing, uses them for its own purposes, the protestor is left with only a growing sense of inadequacy and frustration.

Youth's search for self in permissive sex, as Nicholi suggests, also creates further frustration. There is something about the mystery of sex that debases the self who illicitly invades the sexuality of another. Sex lies deep in the structure of the self, for it is a reflection of the self's creation in the image of God. Nicholi is right: When sex comes easy, the value of sex is reduced, and with this reduction comes a greater dissatisfaction with the self, for sex belongs to the essence of the self.

WHAT IS MAN?

The search for identity is nothing new. For centuries man has pursued the Socratic dictum: Know thyself. The mystery of the human person is indicated by the variety of theories advanced. It has been urged that man in essence is a rational being, a religious being, a tool-making being, a romantic being, an evolving biological being, an existential being whose essence lies in freedom, a purely material determined being and a psychological being (variously defined). And the search for the self continues.

The dissent and protest of modern youth is directed against a social structure and economic orientation in which men exist more for things than things for men. But men are more than things, as life is more than clothing. Today's youth is saying, "Up with people." Yet, aside from the worthy result of seizing the consciences of many people, the youth protest movement has not been very effective. It has brought some changes and improvements in the social order. But as far as restoring the human self to its proper place on the scale of values, it has accomplished little. No doubt this stems in part from its own failure to discover with certainty just what and who a human person is.

Like so many earlier assayists of the human self, these protesters fail to discover the true nature of our *humanitas* because they seek the clue to the self within the self, or, as in permissive sex, within another human self. But the mystery of the self does not lie in the self. It lies rather in man's origin and in the divine image according to which he was patterned. As one created by God in God's image, the very reality of the self is a thing of mystery and wonder. It is not a mysterious thing that God exists. Christians can think of God as the only-existent, who created nothing. But that other selves, human selves, exist, this for the Christian is a mysterious and wondrous thing! Sexuality is one facet of the mystery and wonder. Belonging to each other as members of a single humanity, belonging to each other in marriage in such a way that, in Paul's words, "he that loveth his wife loveth himself," belonging to each other in the church as members of Christ's Body and members of each other (a concept of membership that never arose in paganism and is little recognized today), belonging to God so that God is literally *my,* or *our* God, this too is the mystery and wonder of our reality as individual selves and community.

Neither modern protesting youth nor their more complacent elders will ever discover the authentic nature of human selfhood and personhood and the kind of society appropriate to human beings apart from a reference that transcends humanity. Socrates spent his life studying the human self, but he never settled in his own mind whether man was a demonic or a god-like being. Emerson did no better, for he studied man and concluded that "man is a god in ruins." Calvin took the biblical teaching about man seriously and concluded, "It is certain that man never achieves a clear knowledge of himself unless he has first looked upon God's face, and then descends from contemplating him to scrutinize himself." Indeed, Calvin *begins* his

Institutes by asserting that the true knowledge of God and the true knowledge of man are so interrelated that we cannot have the one without the other.

Nicholi, as I hear him, is saying that the arrows of protest sent out by young people either fall broken to the ground or turn upon the sender and make him their target. There is only one way out of this frustrating and self-defeating aggression. It is only before God that youth, from behind its whiskers, granny glasses and patched jeans, will be able to discover its real self and the authentic forms of community.

The Loss and Recovery of the Personal
by James M. Houston

The notion of what is personal is a vast subject. Indeed all the fundamental problems of what it means to be human are present in the problem of persons and the personal. These notions are central to the field of ethics. Ethics might almost be defined as the study of what it means to be a person and therefore to have those qualities of life that we describe as the personal. Psychology, too, investigates the domain of the personal in terms of what is meant by personality, employing the two indispensable ideas of integration and uniqueness. The psychological view of the personal thus refers, on the one hand, to the functioning of the whole person in expressing his individual needs, and, on the other hand, to his social relationships. Most commonly, the psychological view of the personal refers to how an individual functions as a recognizable unity, with distinctive traits, drives, attitudes and habits which enable or prevent his attaining an adequate adjustment to his environment and to himself. The personal, too, is now viewed as a particular philosophical stance towards reality, such as in Michael Polanyi's theory of personal knowledge or in John Macmurray's logic of the personal. In brief, all the fundamental problems of man are present in the personal, but it may well be that their solution is also present within the same area of reflection.

The primary meaning of the term *personal* according to the Oxford Dictionary is "that pertaining to, concerning or affecting the individual person or self." When it is used to denote what set of qualities distinguish one person from another, confusion often exists between the use of the terms *personal* and *personality*. This definition of "personal individuality" should be used in connection with the term *personality,* that is, the "otherness" of each individual as differentiated from other people. The term *personal* has a wider meaning. For the personal is not an isolate. It is the field in which we know one another as persons in personal relationships. Thus it is truly defined as the personal attitudes we have to other persons. These personal attitudes are themselves known not by conceptual knowledge, itself impersonal, but by relational knowledge, the experience of personal relationships.

THE LOSS OF THE PERSONAL
If the definition of what is personal is an elusive concept, since it must be experienced to be known, the loss of the personal is likewise a vast and complex field of investigation affecting our whole awareness of life and of what it means to be human.

In an essential sense, the loss of the personal is the fate of all mankind as fallen beings. Some unfortunate human beings, never having been treated as persons, do not know what it is to be personal. In some measure or other we all suffer some impairment of personal relationship which mars or distorts our capacity to be personal. The quality and possibility of "personalness" is always relative and always capable of further improvement. Thus at the very outset, what it means to be personal is threatened by indefinability, both by our limited experience of it and by the impossibility of defining personal experience of it in conceptual terms. Nevertheless we are driven forward to explore it by the awareness that our concern for persons is of particular concern for us as human beings. We respond positively to the slogan that "people matter more than things" or that "love is the greatest thing in the world." Here is a realm of intrinsic worth.

Beyond the experience that personal relations are impaired

by living in an imperfect world, there is a deep and widespread anxiety that the loss of the personal is being precipitated by accelerating forces in our technological society. These forces are so complex and circular in their interrelationships of cause and effect that at best we can only refer to the problem as "the ecology of depersonalization." We can all single out individual features that reveal in our selection the subjectivity of our own views. Erich Fromm has summarized it as an era "in which men are transformed into things and become appendices to the process of production and consumption." Paul R. Ehrlich, writing as a prophet of doom about the dire consequences of world overpopulation by 1975, quotes the old Chinese proverb that states: "It is hard to tell the difference between right and wrong when the belly is empty." Ehrlich adds, "As serious as world tensions are today, consider what they will be like when almost everyone is hungry and nations are competing for increasingly scarce food resources." Others fear most of all the threat of biopsychological techniques which would manipulate the memory of man and his genetic characteristics, and leave him at the mercy of brain controllers. As Jean Rostand said, "Science has made us Gods before we are even worthy of being men."

From a Christian perspective, Jacques Ellul has given a pessimistic analysis of his pronouncement that "at present there is no counterbalance to technique." In previous societies a number of different forces played a restraining role. There have been the rules of precise conduct covered by the term *morality.* Close to it has been *public opinion,* a set of much more irrational reactions, not necessarily related to what is good or bad for man and society. And there has been *social structure,* also reacting strongly to whatever new factors might threaten it. Finally, there has been the *state,* the special organ of defense of a society. Today, argues Ellul, our society is completely orientated towards technique as the instrument of performance, of power, of man's worship. So far has this worship, or what we may call "technolatry," gone that there is a deep conviction that technical problems are the only serious problems of society, so that public opinion, the social structure and the state are all orientated towards technology. In consequence, man no longer has any means by which to subjugate technique to himself; rather he is demeaned so that man is subservient to technology. Man tends no longer to be a person; rather he is appraised by the techniques he represents in his training, as a scientist, philosopher, artist, mechanic or typist.

With the assumption that technical progress is inevitable and cannot be checked by moral sanctions, public opinion, social structure or the state, the technocratic prophets of the future, such as Alvin Toffler in *Future Shock,* exhibit an incredible naivete about the scientific golden age ahead of us: gene banks; a super race; the irrelevance of the family; the technical efficiency that reshapes at will human emotions and human values, and forbids men to have children, to be religious, even to be human. They appear unaware of the terrifying totalitarianism they are seeking to introduce, one that will be more dehumanizing than the bloody dictatorships of Stalin and Hitler.

The cult of scientism and its concomitant development of technolatry invite the loss of the personal in the area of privacy. Techniques themselves already threaten more improvements in the technology of eavesdropping: photographs from afar, concealed microphones, closed-circuit television, tapped telephone lines and much else. Another threat is the increased pressure on people to surrender their privacy as recipients of the government's overexpanding welfare benefits. It becomes less and less easy to resist government claims to a widening amount of information about our personal character, living habits and family knowledge. There is also the rapid progress of record-keeping, of collating information about individuals which is permanently stored in computers. Commitments to social science research are creating ever new penetrations of the privacy of the individual so that in such spheres as sexology the domain of privacy is now explored publicly. The uses of drugs, hypnosis, contact therapy and personality tests are robbing man of his dignity as a person, neutralizing him and objectifying him to the status of an animal to be understood in deterministic terms. In a few decades "the imperialism of the social sciences may well have claimed a large part of the private domain"—this is the conclusion drawn by Harry Kalven in a study on this issue.

Concomitant with this is the decline of family life. Throughout man's history, the family has been the citadel of the personal. It provided an institution where private things were shared and set a boundary point beyond which things were no one else's business. What is characteristic of the family is that it is neither established by force nor maintained by a sense of duty. It is established and nurtured by loyalty and natural affection. Care for one another is sufficient to hold it together; neither fear nor domination is necessary. The loss of loyalty by the affluence of choices, by the multiplicity of personal contacts in a metropolitan world, by the diverse interests of age groups, professional groups, sexes and peer groups and by all the distractions of our contemporary world, has sapped the vitality and coherence of family life. Too many of our contemporaries have lost sight of the reality that loyalty is the foundation of morality and of the personal.

With the loss of the family values there is the intensification of urbanism, that interpenetration of technology and city life that erodes not only personal privacy and family life but also personal values. In the city, values are pluralistic; the morals and cultures of men jostle with each other in an ethical kaleidoscope of confusion and often clash in violence and crime. Lacking solitude and peace, the mass-mindedness of the urbanite creates what David Riesman has called the outer-directedness of individuals who have lost their roots, their deep convictions and commitments. The city, then, is the sphere of "the persuaders," those advertising agents, members of the mass media and others whose task is to turn society into a cosmic digestive system of consumers. The distinctive values and faith of the individual are overlooked for the lowered average values of humanity en masse. The moral danger of mass-mindedness is its indifference to moral standards and personal values, an indifference that leads to an atrophy of character that is as apathetic of feelings as the efficiency of a well-run broiler house. Existentialism and such recent phenomena as the theatre of the absurd are manifest protestations against this malaise of mass-mindedness.

The loss of the personal is also a reflection of the rise of individualism, that egocentric stance of private interests and private morals. It is a denial of the ecological web of personal relationships and of the need for community. It is basically an economic phenomenon, now being spread the world over by technology and material affluence. The cult of individualism is itself the consequence of the dissolving ties of family life and of other basic groupings based on loyalty and reverence. And it is in city life where the material and depersonalized values are at their most intensive state. Therein is the milieu, the vacuum of basic values, for the proliferation of mass-mindedness. In turn, it is in this personalized authority of mass-mindedness that totalitarianism rises on fertile ground for the opposite result of individualism, the tyranny of the dictator.

Behind these forces of depersonalization is the overweening authority placed on science as the prime field of reflection, instead of only a limited field. It is the Cartesian doctrine writ large over our whole world that "I think therefore I am"—the objective and impersonal stance towards life. The error is not in the scientific account of life but of our false valuation of the objective attitude as the only norm for all possible attitudes. It is assumed that it is the only and complete account of reality and that therefore the religious dimension has little or no real significance as a dimension of life. These areas of dependence, awe and fear, traditionally the realm of the religious, are being usurped by man's dependence on technology. His sense of being a creature is vanishing, and his arrogance as a creator is being powerfully reinforced. Moreover, technocratic man is preoccupied with limited, practical ends so that he tends to eschew ultimate questions and even their credibility is becoming suspect. As Bernard Meland has said in *The Secularization of Mod-*

ern Cultures, "The men who work in laboratories on specific projects, especially when they are engaged in projects allied with industry, think and move within a sphere of knowledge and purpose which is expressive of immediate cycles of cause and effect, and nothing more." The tyranny of the scientific mood is the sense of determinism and the realm of the empirical. The influence then of technology is seemingly inimical to reflection upon ultimate questions and indeed to the very faculty of reflection itself.

THE RECOVERY OF THE PERSONAL

Thus the Christian must start by questioning the all-sufficiency of the technologist's empiricism and the intellectual posture of scientism. The initial task of confronting the dehumanizing tendencies of modern life must be to emphasize that the religious life is the life of the personal, of how and why personal relations are of ultimate concern. Science cannot monopolize life, as the scientist knows very well when he leaves his laboratory to greet his wife. To avert the theory-centered and egocentric predicament of man, we must turn from the definition of man, "I think therefore I am," to an action-oriented stance, "I respond therefore I am." This is the Christian view of life, that faith is active and also communal or interpersonal. Faith is the authentic stance for awareness of ourselves as persons, dependent upon others and having character from others. Religion for the Christian is that total experience of the whole personality of man that characterizes his humanness. To be faithful to his nature, he needs to be personal. To be personal, he needs faith. Augustine recognized that God "exists more truly than He is thought" and that "we believe in order to know, we do not know in order to believe."

Even Christians need to dehellenize their attitudes to life and faith, not that they need to do so historically (for this is an impossibility), but they need to do so philosophically. For the biblical view of life is that there is no atomization of life, no science of theology distinct from the action of God. God is a

living God related primarily to the events of creation and redemption, not of conceptuality. As Johannes Pedersen has
shown in *Israel: Its Life and Culture,* the God who speaks is the
God who acts, and he is revealed in action-orientated not con-
cept-orientated terms. Thus the Old Testament is not a collec-
tion of static theological doctrines but rather a dynamic testi-
mony of the community of men in their living relation to the
absolute Other. There is no Hebrew word *to think*; there is no
inactive thinking. Always the function of thinking is in its relation to the appropriate action. "As a man thinketh so is he."
Thought is the eyes of action. God therefore is not a theological
proposition but Agent and Action.

Because the Hebrew view of man is also as a totality—life that
eats, speaks and acts—human intercourse is the expression of
such life. Blessing is impossible without intercourse, and intercourse is impossible without the family. As Pedersen says, "Man
is only what he is as a link in the family. He derives his life from
the family, shares it with the family." The family is the fundamental factor of life, and the book of Ruth is a beautiful testi-
mony to this principle, expressed in the virtue of loyalty.

Sin is therefore "that wrong which breaks fellowship between
persons. Whatever brings two persons into contradiction or
opposition with one another is sin." Likewise, it is through the
logic of the personal that the whole force of Christian revelation
meets us: of God as personal, of our need of him, of our need
for reconciliation and forgiveness, of Christ as personal identity,
significance and security, and of the awareness of the Christian
community in our brother for whom Christ died. The more
there is this sense of the loss of the personal, the more obvious
should become our sense of its recovery in Christ.

II
The Self & the Community

The Self and the Community
by D. Elton Trueblood

The most important fact which we know about the universe is that it has persons in it. Each finite person is an occasion for hope and also a potential danger, because it is of the very nature of the personal reality that it should be unstable and even liable to self-destruction. The rock cannot destroy itself by a false conception of its meaning, but persons can do this and have, in fact, done so in many instances. The recent visits of men to the moon have made more vivid what we already knew about the amazing stability of rocks. The sample stones brought back to earth by the men of Apollo 15 appear not to have changed at all during the thousands of years when the life of persons has been changing all of the time. It is because persons are beings who are engaged in the emergence of novelty that perfect historical prediction is impossible.

We often hear the complaint that we do much worse in human development than we do in scientific development and that an equal expenditure of money would alter the disparity, but the complaint is fundamentally naive. Of course it is harder to manage persons than it is to manage atoms, because atoms have no freedom and therefore no sin. The management of human life is not only difficult and disappointing, but also exhilarating, and it will always be so because of the kind of reality with which we are dealing. Much of the instability of human organization arises from the relationship between the self and the community, the emphasis upon both of these being necessary for the authentic development of personhood. Civilizations are essentially unstable formations because they are created and sustained by beings who are always oscillating between two poles.

REINHOLD NIEBUHR'S ANALYSIS

My own interest in the question of the right ordering of the claims of personal identity and social responsibility was much enhanced by the West Lectures delivered by Reinhold Niebuhr at Stanford University early in 1944. I had the good fortune to be Professor Niebuhr's host and to be able to rejoice in the splendid reception accorded the lectures, which were later published with the title *The Children of Light and the Children of Darkness.* The book, which may be rightly regarded as the most brilliant work of a brilliant Christian thinker, was given the subtitle *A Vindication of Democracy and a Critique of Its Traditional Defense.* Since the death of Professor Niebuhr has recently occurred, I am glad to envisage my essay as a slight recognition of personal indebtedness to him. The subject of this essay was one very familiar to Niebuhr, his second and crucial lecture in the series being entitled "The Individual and the Community."

Central to Reinhold Niebuhr's analysis was the recognition of the inadequacy of the familiar secular defenses of democratic theory, especially those which stem from the doctrine of Rousseau. I suppose it was Niebuhr who first made me see that the Christian thinkers have, on the whole, been far more sophisticated in their handling of the problems of democracy than have the pure secularists. Having as their support the doctrine of original sin, Christian thinkers have often been able to avoid the twin dangers of according too much power to the isolated individual and too much power to the collective. Above all, the ideal of self-sufficiency can easily be recognized, in Christian philosophy, as both untrue and politically dangerous. "The ideal of self-sufficiency, so exalted in our liberal culture," said Niebuhr, "is recognized in Christian thought as one form of the primal sin. For self-love, which is the root of all sin, takes two social forms. One of them is the domination of other life by the self. The second is the sin of isolationism" (*The Children of Light,* p. 55).

The crucial mistake is concentrating on one set of perils while neglecting the opposite ones. In short, the true way is narrow and there are wide gutters on both sides. It is no gain if, in a determined effort to stay out of one gutter, a person falls into the opposite one. Error comes by failure to recognize that danger is multiple. This seems to be the practical significance of Christ's warning about the double danger in the words, "Beware of the leaven of the Pharisees and the leaven of Herod" (Mk. 8:15). Reinhold Niebuhr caught our attention when he said, "Preoccupation with the perils of collective forms of ambition produces social theories which emphasize freedom at the expense of order, ending finally in the philosophy of anarchism. Preoccupation with the perils of individual inordinateness, on the other hand, allows the fear of anarchy to bear the fruit of connivance with tyranny" (*The Children of Light,* p. 47).

It is obvious, when we think about it, that total concentration on either the self or the community is destructive of human values. The cult of individualism, if consistently applied, would make any genuine civilization impossible. This is because the really separated individual would not be able either to learn from others or to pass on to others any accumulated wisdom about life. We can see something of the potential danger in the recently popular and thoroughly vulgar admonition, "Do your own thing." Taken seriously, this admonition would make persons into separated monads uninfluenced by one another. There would be no value in history and no possibility of group creation of the future. Indeed, all concern for the welfare of others would be undermined. Freedom is an undoubted value, but unless there is some limitation upon it, all other values are destroyed. Absolute freedom would mean absolute chaos.

The whole idea of the totally separated individual, following rules of his own making, is an idea which could not possibly be given embodiment. In any case, such an individual would not be a person and would represent an inner contradiction, for the wholly separated being is not even a self. Those who advocate uninhibited self-expression are really proposing an impossible dream. The completely separate self is a contradiction in terms, for if there is no consciousness of others, there is no self-consciousness. Important as the conception of personal identity may be, it cannot stand alone.

At the same time, the merely collective person is an intrinsic impossibility. Ants, as we all know, can do marvelous things, and they do them by collective efficiency. In Uganda I once saw an ant hill that was actually fourteen feet high. No ant, working alone, could possibly produce anything of this kind, but ants can do it as a community. It is important to recognize, however, that they pay a high price for their collective efficiency; they do not become persons at all! That development in this direction is a real danger for humans is shown by some features of life in modern China. History might, conceivably, move in this direction, but the consequent tragedy would be immense.

We are making a start on the philosophy of civilization when we realize that both individualism and collectivism represent flights from reality, for the real is neither the separated nor the undifferentiated. Just as the mere individual is an abstraction, so the mere community has no counterpart in reality. Society means nothing unless it is composed of individuals, each possessing his own dignity and enjoying his own rights. The way of wisdom, therefore, is to hold both conceptions in dynamic tension. Whenever we relieve the tension, settling simplistically for one or the other, we are already lost.

When we see the faddish swings of the pendulum in contemporary experience, we realize that the problem of the self and the community is by no means a merely academic one. Both extremes are observed every day, some persons being so confused that they actually demonstrate both errors in their own behavior. It is not uncommon, for instance, to encounter persons who, on one side, loudly affirm their right to express their individuality with no limitations, while, on the other side, they exhibit a servile conformity in dress, speech, choice of music and general manner of life. The fact that the contradiction is not recognized to be such is part of the disease. It is a revelation of the triumph of irrationality.

A recognition of both the danger and the disease helps·us to appreciate the role of the Christian intellectual. It is part of the task of Christians in the modern world to give real leadership, especially in the overcoming of confusion. The problem of modern man, in his oscillation between the two poles of self and community, is by no means a new one for the thoughtful Christian. Long ago a sophisticated answer was worked out and it is a highly satisfactory one. It is the duty of thoughtful Christians not merely to tend their own spiritual gardens but to share their insights and thus give assistance to mankind in general. Our responsibility is not primarily to the minority who are committed Christians, but to the vast majority of those who have no such commitment. This is part of what is meant by the penetration of the world which is represented by the metaphor of leaven. It is not sufficient for us to operate as a remnant, separated from the world. If there is something which is revealed, it is our duty to spread it as widely as possible. Our conviction is that the problem of the self and the community is one in regard to which some genuine light is available.

1793430

THE GREAT CHRISTIAN WORD

Always the great Christian word is *and*. In a number of situations the Christian insight is that *either-or* produces a heresy while *and* can bring us close to reality. Examples of this in the Gospels are numerous. The Great Commandment, as we all know, is a double one, involving not only the insight of Deuteronomy 6:5 but also that expressed in Leviticus 19:18. The originality lies in the conjuction of what must not be separated and in the consequent emergence of the paradox of double priority. The love of God is not real without the love of the brethren, and the love of the brethren is not real without the love of God. A similar use of the "holy conjunction" is that regarding the new and the old (Mt. 13:52). That this wisdom is greatly needed in our contemporary culture is indicated by the way in which the masses swing mindlessly between the conformities of conservatism and the conformities of modernism. It is Christ's clear teaching that both new and old are required and that they are required together. Much foolishness about the claims of piety and the claims of social action could be overcome if the wisdom involved in the use of the holy conjunction were understood and followed.

The more we delve into the Scriptures the more we understand the conjunctive genius of the Christian faith. One facet which is quickly illuminated is that of prayer. There is obviously a time when a person ought to pray alone, and this he will do if he follows Christ's own example, for we know that he went alone into a solitary place. But we also know that he prayed with others and even asserted that it was in the fellowship that his presence would be available. To settle for mere aloneness or mere togetherness is to miss the magnitude for which Christ calls. Another use of conjunction in prayer is represented by the equal emphasis upon spirituality and intelligence. The Apostle Paul brings his remarkable good sense to bear on the issue by saying "I will pray as I am inspired to pray, but I will also pray intelligently" (1 Cor. 14:15, NEB).

Beginning with the glory of *and* which is intrinsic to the gospel, Christian experience through the centuries has refined the conception, which is now applicable not merely to Christians but to all persons, that the self needs the community and that the community needs the self. On the one hand, there is abundant emphasis upon what is valid in individuality. The validity lies not in the fatuous belief that the individual is ever self-sufficient, but in the fact that the individual is always important. Each one is one and each is precious because each is the object of the divine concern. The notion that each person, regardless of race or sex or age or learning, is intrinsically valuable is one of the most revolutionary ideas in the world. When fully appreciated, it is bound to undermine all unfair discrimination and inequality of opportunity. This conception is not tied to the clearly erroneous belief that all people are equal in intelligence or in ability. If it were, it would be doomed at the start, because factual inequality is part of the obvious truth about human life. In one sense, it is the foundation stone in Plato's social edifice and has been understood widely by his thoughtful successors in subsequent generations.

The Christian idea of all men being "created" equal, which found its way into the American Declaration of Independence, is the profound idea that each individual is equally precious in God's eyes. Each, in spite of differences and in spite of factual inequality of powers, is made in God's image. Not a sparrow falls without the Father's affectionate concern, yet persons are far more precious than sparrows. It is no wonder, then, that the Divine Shepherd goes out to seek the *one* that is lost. In short, as Christians see reality, persons are not merely items in a mass called humanity, but each is single as an object of affection. The love of humanity is always an abstraction and sometimes an affectation, since the only adequate object of affection is the individual person.

Herein lies the rational appeal of the familiar doctrine of the dignity of the individual, which is always a derivative doctrine. It does not mean, of course, that persons are ultimately separate, but it does mean that persons are ultimately valuable. Therefore, we must ask of every proposal for social progress, "What will it do to persons?" In dealing with the race problem we must ask how individual dignity can be enhanced and maintained. The most terrible thing about human slavery while it lasted was that for great numbers of human beings it destroyed any possibility of individual dignity.

While the Christian understanding of personal reality has stressed the individual, it has also stressed equally the community. Herein lies one of the most striking contrasts between Christianity and several of the other religions which have emerged in world history. From the beginning, it was recognized that it is not possible to be a Christian alone, for it is only in the fellowship that the new life can be known. So well was this understood in primitive Christianity that the redemptive fellowship arose even before the New Testament was produced. In fact, much of the New Testament was produced because of the felt needs of the existing fellowships. Community was not something which was added to the Christian revelation, but was something intrinsic to it. That is part of what is involved in the affirmation "Something bigger than the temple is here" (Mt. 12:6). A great deal of what went on at the Temple in Jerusalem, like that which transpired at the Parthenon, was individual religion.

In so far as we realize that it is impossible to be a Christian alone, we recognize the necessity of the church, for the church is simply the Christian community. How easily this point may be missed we can see by reference to one of the greatest of twentieth-century philosophers, Alfred North Whitehead. I owe much to this good man, with whom I had a warm personal relationship. He was both humble and kind, demonstrating in his own life many of the specific Christian virtues. I can never forget how I sat and listened to his now famous Lowell Lectures which, when they were published in 1926, were entitled *Religion in the Making*. I was impressed, of course, as a very young man, with his practical conception of the role of philosophy. "If my view of the function of philosophy is correct," he wrote in his preface to the first set of Lowell Lectures, "it is the most effective of all the intellectual pursuits. It builds cathedrals before the workmen have moved a stone, and it destroys them before the elements have worn down their arches." This is heady stuff, and, young as I was, I knew that I was fortunate in being able to sit at the feet of a genuine sage.

What is most surprising about Whitehead's one specifically religious book is that its most quoted sentence is clearly wrong. Religion, the great man said, is what a man does with his solitariness. This is an excellent illustration of the conception that error is truth in isolation. Whitehead's mistake lay not in emphasizing one pole but in emphasizing it without equal reference to the other pole. Whatever religion Whitehead was referring to in his famous definition, he was certainly not referring to Christianity, for the definition would eliminate the church, and Christianity without the church would be something utterly foreign to what we have experienced.

Christian thinkers have recognized all along that their proposed solution of the problem of the self and the community involves genuine paradox. At first view, self-sufficiency and responsibility to others seem to be incompatible. Even the child in Sunday School feels something of the tension which is involved in two texts which appear close together in the New Testament. How can we reconcile "Bear one another's burdens" (Gal. 6:2) and "Each man will have to bear his own load" (Gal. 6:5)? This is, indeed, a paradox, but it is part of the sophistication of Christian thinking that paradox is necessary to the expression of whatever is profound. We dare not refer to the greatness of man unless we refer, equally and contemporaneously, to the littleness of man. Herein lies the immense appeal of the famous opening lines of A Tale of Two Cities. Dickens avoided being simplistic about the period of the French Revolution by beginning: "It was the best of times, it was the worst of times."

There is a deep sense in which each man must carry his own load, for no other person fully understands what the load is. We shall never have a good society if people expect to be pensioners of a welfare state with all services being rendered for them, but, unless we also feel responsibility for the needs of others, we are not really persons at all. This is the truth, as Christians see it, but we claim that it is really truth for everybody, for it has already received ample verification. There is good reason to think, then, that it applies to the industrial, the academic and the political orders, and not merely to some fragment of life denoted the religious order.

One of the best contributions which Christian thought can make to the thought of the world is the repetition of the reminder that life is complex. It is part of the Christian understanding of reality that all simplistic answers to basic questions are bound to be false. Over and over, the answer is *both-and* rather than *either-or*. The fact that there is validity in the appeal of individual liberty does not mean there is any lack of validity in the appeal of the community. Only by keeping both in mind do we have a modicum of insurance against either anarchy or tyranny. The uninhibited libertarian is as much a menace as is the totalitarian, and vice versa. Modern democratic theory tends, unfortunately, to oscillate between two necessary ideals, each of which is valuable in conjunction but damaging in isolation. It is part of the vocation of the Christian intellectual to utter at least two warnings at once. There must be, on the one hand, a warning against any individualism which makes the separated person his own end, but there must be, at the same time, a warning against any collectivism which regards the community as the end of the individual.

A Hard Look at the Church
by David Carley

This conference has been titled "A Christian Perspective on the Search for Reality in Modern Life." By definition, the "search for reality" means not only a search for the real in life, or perhaps even for an ideal, but also a willingness first to find out the truth about ourselves—in this instance, to find out the truth about ourselves as individuals and as persons collected together in communities.

A SERIOUS CHARGE

Professor Trueblood has called the now well-known phrase "Do your own thing" a "thoroughly vulgar admonition." Implicitly, I think, he attributes this ideal to the current advocates of the counter culture. My charge is far more serious. I believe that by our actions, by our life styles and by what we do rather than what we say, the majority of Christians in America today have concern for little other than ourselves; that the concept of community is mostly foreign to our patterns of living; and that the great paradox Trueblood refers to is only a conceptual one for most of us because, in reality, the paradox between choosing self-sufficiency or the good of the whole is hardly a good wrestling match. The self wins almost every time.

A working definition of community includes but goes beyond local community to encompass religion, work, family and culture. It refers to social bonds characterized by emotional cohesion, depth, continuity and fullness. James Gustafson has said that "it refers to a body of persons who share some measure of common life, and a common loyalty."[1] He says elsewhere that the "loyalty is commitment" and also that "communal loyalty is expressed in action." Finally he says, "The moral penetration of the other communities to which Christians belong through their vocations is an expression of the *community of deed*" (emphasis mine).[2]

Sadly, as I see it, there is little "moral penetration" of existing American culture and institutions by Christians, who, through exerting a self-conscious commitment and positive *action,* could hardly fail to influence strongly our present culture.

In the fifth of the famous West Lectures at Stanford in 1944 (the same lectures which Trueblood has quoted from in his paper), Reinhold Niebuhr says: "The insistence of the Christian faith that the love of Christ is the final norm of human existence must express itself socially in unwillingness to stop short of the whole human community in expressing our sense of moral responsibility for the life and welfare of others. The understanding of the Christian faith that the highest achievements of human life are infected with sinful corruption will help men to be prepared for new corruptions on the level of world community which drive simpler idealists to despair. The hope of Christian faith that the divine power which bears history can complete what even the highest human striving must leave incomplete, and can purify the corruptions which appear in even the purest human aspirations, is an indispensable prerequisite for diligent fulfillment of our historic tasks."[3]

If this were a conference of monks, working in lonely isolation from the world in quest of a new *Summa Theologica,* or indeed if this were the world of Niebuhr's great lecture series in the mid-war mid-forties, we might be content to discuss the paradox in intellectual terms of self-sufficiency versus community.

But this is the nihilist-like American generation of the 1970s in which we Christians find ourselves, and we are contending with the realities of loneliness, guilt, alienation, anomie and the nuclear family. We have a commitment to Jesus Christ, which in turn involves the acceptance of a mission and a purpose which leads to action. Again to quote Gustafson, "The Christian community consists of those who are loyal to Jesus Christ as the contributing person and event of the Christian history. Christians believe in Him; they bring life under the interpretation of the meaning of this Person. They have an obligation to the community because of this declared loyalty."[4]

Certainly, we as Christians do not endorse B. F. Skinner's engineered community in which man's wants are adjusted through behavioral programming, as in his *Walden Two*. But neither can we accept the totally individualistic doctrine that if man can only free himself from the strictures of his institutional development through family, church, school and place of employment—strictures which are believed to be limiting and unnecessary—then he will naturally grow and develop to a greater state of congruence, genuineness and empathy. (This concept is built on the premise that the individual who is provided with an opportunity to experiment with ideas and behavior can determine who he is rather than depending upon the definition of others for his identity.) But even here, non-Christian psychoanalysts, such as Erik Erikson and others, tell us *that one learns who he is through others*. And therefore, even in the pursuit of identity, man must acknowledge the limitations of the self.

ALL IS NOT WELL

A casual reader might infer from Trueblood's paper that modern-day Christians have only to avoid the excessiveness of individualism and community alike and all will be well; further, that they as Christians are very much concerned with civil and personal rights, personal dignity and personal moral responsibility; additionally, that they as members of society are also concerned and involved in those values that are beyond the self, namely, an abiding concern for their fellowmen, indeed a love for others.

Sadly, the evidence is much to the contrary in my opinion.

Relatively few Christians are self-consciously concerned with the requisites of classic individualism. Too few can ever be found who enlist in the struggle for personal rights and dignity for all human beings and far too few who live lives on the scriptural premise of personal moral responsibility. In terms of the Christian's posture today toward his obligation to the community (in John Gardner's words, "an allegiance to values more comprehensive than his own needs"), again I'm afraid that there is slight evidence.

Protestant Christians may not like it, but many radical Catholics have a greater sense of community today than most of us. The priest brothers Berrigan have demonstrated an awareness of community that I believe many Protestant Christians ought to consider carefully.

John Gardner, in a chapter which is one of the best secular statements I know of on the topic we are discussing, says at the conclusion of the chapter (entitled "Individuality and Its Limits"): "We must also help the individual to discover how such commitments may be made without surrendering individuality. We must help him to understand and resist any impulse he may have to flee the responsibility of individual choice by mindless submission to a Cause or Movement. In short, he must recognize the hazard of having no commitments beyond the self and the hazard of commitments that imperil the self."[5]

---

1. *James Gustafson,* Treasure in Earthen Vessels: The Church as a Human Community *(New York: Harper and Row, 1961), p. 1.*

2. *Ibid., p. 12.*

3. *Reinhold Niebuhr,* The Children of Light and the Children of Darkness *(New York: Charles Scribner's Sons, 1944), pp. 188-89.*

4. *Gustafson, p. 12.*

5. *John Gardner,* Self-Renewal: The Individual and the Innovative Society *(New York: Harper and Row, 1963), p. 95.*

The Failure of a Religious Subculture
by Douglas D. Feaver

Amen! So be it! Part of the "good news" of the Christian is the paradox that in Christ one finds both one's uniqueness and one's need for community met. Thus, and only thus, do we fully attain true personhood. I am eternally grateful to Christian thinkers like Professor Trueblood who have so eloquently affirmed this truth.

The problems we face today, unfortunately, are not merely matters of truth, however, but of life. Propositional truths, like Ultimate Truth, must become incarnate. It is not enough to *say* "Lord! Lord!"; we must *do* "the will of the Father." The fact is, at least as I have seen it from my limited vantage point, that it would be dishonest to claim that there are very many churches in which people are both finding their personal identity and uniqueness affirmed and, at the same time, finding themselves bound into a genuine *koinonia* of the sharing of life, light and love.

Trueblood vividly reminded us of the "gutters" on either side of the Narrow Way—the one of personal piety, the other of social concern. He rightly emphasized the holy conjunctions *both-and,* over against the heretical *either-or.* But I fear the situation today is neither holy nor heretical; instead we have the demonic *neither-nor—neither* genuine personal piety *nor* genuine communal relevance.

Instead of an affirmation of the unique and eternal value of the individual soul (for whom Christ died), there is an oppres-

sive demand for conformity to the norms of a religious subculture (whether this subculture is *avant-garde* or *devant-garde*),
and yet submission to the demands for conformity does not
ensure acceptance into a genuine community of concern.

TWO STRIKING FACTS

This is what lies behind two striking facts about the religious
scene on today's campuses (in fact, in the society as a whole):
People are everywhere leaving churches (of every theological
hue) not to escape religion but to find it. Secondly, to a degree
one could never suspect or predict, they are finding it. From the
Jesus freaks to the charismatic house churches, people are seeking and finding Christ outside the churches. And often as not
the reason adduced is precisely this: In the churches they have
found neither personal piety nor communal concern, neither
God nor a brother.

Many of these, perhaps most, are heretical, in Trueblood's
sense of opting for one side of the either-or. In the search for
community we have Christian communes or even Protestant
evangelical (!) nunneries. In the search for a valid experience
with Christ and his Holy Spirit, there have arisen a bewildering
variety of "do it yourself" religions. There can be no doubt that
many of these have in fact "found Christ." Then others, trag-
ically, are woefully (and perhaps fatally) deficient. But the sad
fact is that the situation is not really any better in the main-line
churches or even in the fundamentalistic, independent churches.

We are all one in Christ—yet the Christian churches are the
most segregated institutions in society, alienated not from the
world but from each other, in and out of the congregation. The
racial form of this is only one symptom of a far more pervasive
cancer, expressed in economic, educational, political and now
generational segregation.

But I am not a cynic. I not only believe in the gospel, and
that part of it which our topic discusses, I believe and have seen
it in glorious vindication. In Christ (if not in the visible church),
one does find the only ultimate affirmation of the Personal; and

in him (again, if not in the visible church), one does find oneself bound in a body of concern.

To whom else can we go? Only Christ has the words of eternal life, and he constantly vindicates himself. To him, even if not to his church, I can refer, and have referred, the drug dropout, the rebellious youth, the desperate wife, the helpless widow, and I have seen their needs met. On the other hand, all of these I have seen turned off and turned out—in fact, even exploited—by the visible church. This is one of the reasons for the blossoming of "churches-in-the-home" where genuine experience of Christ is coupled with a viable community of concern.

III

The Real & the Rational

Marcuse, Reich and the Rational
by Ronald H. Nash

The difficulties of attempting a philosophical analysis of any movement as diverse and amorphous as the counter culture are obvious. I have decided to select two authors, Herbert Marcuse and Charles Reich, and let them represent the movement.[1] There are certain advantages, I think, to this approach. First, while it is rather generous to use the word "argument" to refer to the potpourri of half-truths and hasty generalizations that Marcuse and Reich offer in support of their positions (when they even bother to support them), at least these two authors, unlike many they represent, articulate a position in sentences having subjects and predicates. While there are exceptions in Marcuse's case, many of these sentences can even be understood and evaluated. Secondly, each man represents a different segment of the counter culture. Reich speaks for the more passive adherents of the love generation, those who specialize in dropping out. Marcuse speaks for the activist proponents of the hate generation, those who specialize in dropping bombs. Thirdly, both men have become celebrities—in both the counter culture and straight society. Reich's book, *The Greening of America,* was on the best-seller lists for months; Marcuse's books are read by thousands, both within and outside the academic community.

There is hardly time to notice more than a fragment of what Marcuse and Reich have written. I believe, however, that this fragment will be a central and pivotal element of their thought.

I propose to concentrate on certain facets of an epistemological and ethical relativism that is common to both men, as well as to the counter culture they represent. This relativism holds some interesting implications as to their view of reason. I shall conclude by arguing that the implications of this relativism undermine their criticisms of American society and their defense of their own position. Incidentally, nothing I say in this paper should be construed as suggesting that there are not valid criticisms of American society. My point is, if those criticisms are to be sound, one must avoid taking a certain stance toward reason.

I believe it is clear that there is a general distrust or dismissal of reason throughout the counter culture. Marcuse and Reich are hardly extremists in *this* regard, but if we can succeed in showing that their more moderate views lead to absurd or self-defeating consequences, how much more should the views of those who reject reason in the name of subjective feeling or the revolution be repudiated.

THE LAW OF NON-CONTRADICTION

I invite you to consider with me certain fundamental questions about reason, about logic, to be even more specific, about the law of non-contradiction. For example, do the premises of Marcuse and Reich permit the possibility of knowledge and valid inference? I believe I can show that the allegedly devastating critique that Marcuse has made of American society (a critique that recurs frequently in the writings of the counter culture)[2] is self-defeating. That is, if Marcuse's critique were sound, there would have been no possible way in which he could have discovered its soundness. Marcuse's thesis is such that if just one person discovers its truth (and, of course, Marcuse tells us he has), then his thesis must be false.

My own thesis is that any flight from reason, from the canons of logic, is necessarily a flight from reality. When the apologists of the counter culture repudiate logic, they automatically cut themselves off from any possible knowledge of reality. A respect for reason (the law of non-contradiction) is a necessary starting point for any search for truth. Of course this is a very old and very honored philosophical doctrine. Plato used it frequently in his criticisms of the Sophists. Its first systematic formulation is found in Aristotle's *Metaphysics*. I think there is merit, before turning to Marcuse and Reich, in taking a brief look at what Aristotle had to say.

First of all, Aristotle argued for the ontological status of the law of non-contradiction. In other words, the law of non-contradiction is not simply a law of thought. It is a law of thought because it is *first* a law of being. Nor is the law of non-contradiction something you can take or leave. The denial of the law of non-contradiction leads to absurdity. It is impossible meaningfully to deny the laws of logic. If the law of non-contradiction is denied, nothing has meaning including the denial of the law. If the laws of logic do not first mean what they say, nothing else can have meaning. Not only is significant thought impossible if logic is denied, significant action also becomes impossible. Aristotle's statement of this point is classic:

For why does a man walk to Megara and not stay at home thinking he is walking? Why does he not walk early some morning into a well or over a precipice, if one happens to be in his way? Why do we observe him guarding against this, evidently not thinking that falling in is alike good and not good? Evidently he judges one thing to be better and another worse. And if this is so, he must judge one thing to be man and another to be non-man, one thing to be sweet and another to be not-sweet.[4]

In other words, a denial of logic has consequences not only for epistemology and metaphysics but for ethics as well. If all predications are true, there is no difference between walking to a nearby city and walking over a cliff, there is no difference between imbibing LSD and imbibing strontium 90. But obviously there *is* a difference.

Christian theism concurs with this view of reason. Reason and logic have cosmic significance for the Christian. The Christian recognizes that the law of non-contradiction is a law of

being because the universe is the creation of a rational God.
Plato and Aristotle stopped with the postulation of objective
moral and rational order to the universe. Christian theism goes
beyond them and views the rational world as the projection of a
rational God who objectifies his eternal thoughts in his creation.[5]

I submit therefore the following propositions: If the propo-
nent of the counter culture rules out the possibility of valid
inference, he should not expect us to get excited when he
argues for his views or against the views of others. If the propo-
nent of the counter culture tells us that truth is relative, he
should not expect us to accept his truths as absolute. If he tells
us that all beliefs are conditioned by economic and social matters, he should recognize that this vitiates his beliefs as well.

HERBERT MARCUSE AND LIBERATION

Herbert Marcuse is an unsparing critic of all advanced industrial
societies, especially the United States. The details of this critique are not important in this context. What is important is the
question, Why don't the people who live in this corrupt society
do something about it? Marcuse's answer is, They can't. Marx
believed that the workers would carry the revolution. But Marx
could not see how the workers would become part of the Establishment. The worker in an advanced industrial society becomes
corrupted by the affluence of the society until he has the same
values as the bourgeoisie.

Modern technology in societies like our own eliminates dissent and conflict that might arise in less advanced societies. It
does this by raising false needs, providing false satisfactions. It
enslaves people by deceiving them into thinking that the things
it gives them are what they really want—better homes and appli-
ances, faster cars, more leisure and luxury. In effect, you and I
are so completely dominated, controlled, preconditioned, indoctrinated and brainwashed that we cannot even recognize our
bondage. To quote Marcuse's inimitable words (inimitable because there is no one else around who writes like Marcuse),

"The so-called consumer economy and the politics of corporate capitalism have created a second nature of man which ties him libidinally and aggressively to the commodity form." Man becomes so obsessed by the gadgets he wants to possess, handle, consume and renew that he ignores the possibility that this obsession may destroy him. The possibility of man in an advanced industrial society rising up against the hand that feeds him is faint, perhaps nonexistent, because "the second nature of man thus militates against any change that would disrupt and perhaps even abolish this dependence of man on a market ever more densely filled with merchandise."[6]

Marcuse attacks this false mass contentment. The goods produced by the system provide false satisfactions. The system manipulates people into first wanting things and then buying them. And then through such devices as advertising, it increases these wants until the desire to consume becomes compulsive, irrational and inhuman. The belief of the average man that he is happy only shows how total his bondage is. The things that make man think he is happy (the electric can openers, the indoor toilets, the diet colas, the boysenberry-flavored breakfast cereals) are the very chains that bind him. Marcuse knows that we are not really happy. It makes no difference that the individual identifies with his needs and believes they are his. Marcuse knows that the needs are the false products of a repressive society.

What is needed, Marcuse tells us, is for men to free themselves from false needs and false consciousness to true needs and a true consciousness. What is needed is a new type of man who cannot be seduced by affluence.[7] But it is not enough for Marcuse to tell us that men must free themselves from the oppressive influence of false needs imposed by a repressive society; he must tell us how. And more important, he must show us, given his analysis of man's lost estate in the advanced industrial society, that the attainment of liberation and autonomy is possible. It should be clear from what has already been said that this isn't going to be easy.[8] After all, Marcuse makes it clear that there is no way for the system to correct itself because it is impossible for those dominated by the system to free themselves from it. The plot is thickened by two additional ingredients that seem to make liberation impossible.

First, social change cannot take place through democratic means because democracy contributes to the plight of society by lulling people into decisions that are against their best interests. Advanced industrial societies like the United States appear tolerant of minority views because they know that those views cannot have any effect. Men are not free when they vote and make political decisions because all who start out under the domination of a repressive society are preconditioned receptacles; they are incapable of criticizing the society or even heeding a legitimate criticism.

This leads Marcuse to perhaps his most reprehensible doctrine, his view of "Repressive Tolerance."[9] Because our society is in such perilous danger, Marcuse believes the suspension of free speech and free assembly is justified. After all, there is no real value to freedom of speech; it only insures the propagation of lies. Truth is carried by revolutionary minorities (that is, by Marcuse's disciples). Therefore, tolerance should be withdrawn from all those who disagree with Marcuse and extended only to those who make the Great Refusal. Social change must be brought about not by democratic legality but by extra-democratic rebellion. Marcuse wants to replace democratically supported elites with an elite of his own choosing. In Marcuse's words, "Liberating tolerance, then, would mean intolerance against movements from the Right, and toleration of movements from the Left. As to the scope of this tolerance and intolerance . . . it would extend to the stage of action as well as of discussion and propaganda, of deed as well as of word."[10] The funny thing is, Marcuse admits that even if we put these totalitarian measures into practice, even if we destroy existing society, he doesn't know what we'll have.[11] The obvious question here is, How does Marcuse's elite free itself from the conditioning that blinds the rest of us? And who is to save us from the repressiveness of Marcuse's elite? Can anyone be blamed if he sees signs of a neo-Nazi mentality in Marcuse's position?

One of Marcuse's justifications for revolutionary intolerance is the claim that his minority possesses the truth. But what is Marcuse's view of truth? Nowhere in his writings does he tell us what truth is or how man can attain the truth. The truth, he assures us, is not to be identified with what is actual, and he rejects correspondence with fact as a test for truth. He even talks at times as if each age has a different standard of truth. But if truth varies from time to time and from place to place, what reason is there to believe that the words Marcuse pronounces at this time and place are true? What assurance do we have that they will continue to be true the next time he utters them? If you are going to appeal to truth as Marcuse does, you must have a very different view of truth than he possesses.

THE POWERLESSNESS OF CRITICAL SOCIAL THEORY

While the first difficulty in achieving liberation is the failure of the democratic process, the second difficulty is the powerlessness of critical social theory to criticize.[12] The very categories of critical theory were developed within the structure of the system. Furthermore, those who might give the criticism are preconditioned by the system. And finally, those who might otherwise be influenced by a criticism of their society are so brainwashed that they cannot appreciate the force of or understand the nature of the criticism. Thus there is no one to give the critique, no one to understand, and no critical theory in terms of which the needed critique can be given. Things indeed look hopeless. But for whom? Perhaps Marcuse has created a greater problem for himself than he has for capitalism.[13]

But, to quote an old capitalist proverb, things are always darkest just before the dawn. Just when things look the worst, Marcuse begins to see signs of what he calls the Great Refusal all over the place: the revolutions in Vietnam, Cuba and China; guerilla activities in Latin America; strains in the fortress of corporate capitalism; stirrings among ghetto populations; and

last, but not least, student opposition. But there is also a large
and embarrassing lacuna in Marcuse's argument. How, given the
total domination of the repressive society, is this opposition
possible? Does it perhaps come into existence *ex nihilo*?

Let me put my point in another way. Marcuse's thesis is
either what logicians call an A proposition (of the form, All S is
P) or an I proposition (Some S is P). That is, he is either claiming that the repressive influence of capitalist society is all-per-
vasive or that it is only partially effective. If he is claiming that
all people living in advanced industrial societies are controlled,
manipulated and brainwashed to the extent that they think
they are happy, are unable to see their society's faults and are
unable to appreciate criticisms of their society, *then Marcuse's
thesis is self-defeating.* It is self-defeating in the sense that no
one, including himself, could have obtained knowledge of the
thesis. And even granting that Marcuse's books could be the
result of a miracle, no one else, according to this theory, could
have understood him.

But should someone attempt to defend Marcuse by replying
that his thesis is not in fact the A proposition that "All people
in an advanced industrial society are controlled, etc." but only
the I proposition that some are and some are not controlled, his
thesis turns out to be trivial. In any society, you will find some
who are either so stupid or so blinded by ideology, pleasure or
greed that they cannot detect the faults of that system. I have
even met some of Marcuse's disciples who are constitutionally
incapable of understanding the brilliant argument I am presenting. Now it just so happens that Marcuse makes it clear that
his view is indeed the A proposition given above. Listen to what
he says in *One Dimensional Man*: "Technical progress, extended
to a whole system of domination and coordination, creates
forms of life (and of power) which appear to reconcile the
forces opposing the system and to defeat or refute *all* [my
emphasis] protest in the name of the historical prospects of
freedom from toil and domination." Should someone not find
this quotation conclusive, I am quite content to leave him with

the option of deciding whether Marcuse's position is trivial or self-defeating.

There is only time enough to notice one more symptom of what could be called "The Marcuse Syndrome." In *One Dimensional Man* he writes: "The idea of formal logic itself is a historical event in the development of the mental and physical instruments for universal control and calculability. In this undertaking, man had to create theoretical harmony out of actual discord, to purge thought from contradictions, to hypostatize identifiable and fungible units in the complex process of society and nature."[14] Any attempt to interpret Marcuse's tortuous prose involves certain risks. But what he seems to be saying here is patent nonsense. Apparently he believes that history can be divided into two periods. During the A.L. (After Logic) period, men reasoned syllogistically and, generally speaking, observed the logical rules set down by Aristotle. During the B.L. (Before Logic) period, however, men "reasoned" according to principles other than the law of non-contradiction. Forms of reasoning (such as the syllogism logicians call Barbara) which are valid A.L. were invalid B.L. But it is nonsense to talk about a period in history when human "thought" and "reasoning" were not subject to the laws of logic. Marcuse's distinction between thought in accord with logic and "thought" not in accord with logic reduces to a distinction between thought and nonsense. It would be interesting to see Marcuse give us an example of thought not in accord with logic.

CHARLES REICH AND CONSCIOUSNESS III

I'm sure you all have some idea of the distinction Charles Reich's *The Greening of America* makes between Consciousness I, Consciousness II and Consciousness III. "Consciousness I is the traditional outlook of the American farmer, small businessman, and worker who is trying to get ahead. Consciousness II represents the values of an organizational society. Consciousness III is the new generation."[15] The advanced industrial society, the spirit of technology, that Marcuse criticizes is essentially the

Consciousness II that Reich is concerned to attack. Consciousness III is the new stage of consciousness that the coming revolution is producing, a stage that will include a "higher reason" along with a more human community and new, liberated individuals.[16] Reich tells us that the idea of consciousness includes "a person's background, education, politics, insight, values, emotions, and philosophy...."[17] It is clear that Reich means to include logic in the category of philosophy and thus within the category of consciousness. There is no principle of reasoning that transcends all the stages of consciousness.

We are not surprised when still later Reich states, "Each person has his own individuality, not to be compared to that of anyone else. Someone may be a brilliant thinker, but he is not 'better' at thinking than anyone else, he simply possesses his own excellence."[18] No doubt many of Reich's readers were enthralled by this apology for open-mindedness and tolerance. But just consider what he is saying. It almost sounds like that grandfather of all relativists, Protagoras, speaking. Each man is the measure of all things. We must not presume to judge another person's thoughts or beliefs or reasoning. No one's thinking is better than anyone else's. But Reich is not finished. He also informs us that what he calls consciousness is "formed by the underlying economic and social conditions."[19] In other words, a man's culture, politics, philosophy, religion and logic are determined by social and economic conditions.

But there is some question as to whether Reich believes his own position. Consider what he says about Christianity. Christianity, he tells us, has failed for two thousand years and should not be confused with the new generation.

Christianity asks men to give up power, aggression, and materialism for a promise of something better in another world, a world after death.... Unlike Christianity, the new way of life proposes a better life now. It offers something that is immediately more satisfying—the sensual beauty of a creative, loving, unrepressed life. It offers something that is real, not remote. Christianity is just another form of giving up the present for some goal—a religious form of the very repression that characterizes technological man in the Corporate State.[20]

Aside from the unfortunate misrepresentations and Marxist assumptions in this paragraph, it is interesting to wonder what suddenly happened to Reich's tolerance. Apparently one man's thinking is as good as another's except when one happens to be a Christian. But fortunately, Reich has also given the Christian the basis for a reply. Since all beliefs are conditioned by a person's social and economic conditions, Reich's condemnation of Christianity is also conditioned and can thus be conveniently dismissed.

You have to watch these relativists. The moment you turn your back, they begin to absolutize. The same man who has told us that thinking is relative not only from Consciousness to Consciousness but also from person to person actually claims that Consciousness I is more irrational than II while Consciousness II is more irrational than III.[21] Perhaps Reich is in touch with a standard of reason that transcends Consciousness I, II or III. But this, of course, would require him to abandon his relativism. Things are so confusing that it's almost a relief to hear Reich admit that "Consciousness III is deeply suspicious of logic, rationality, analysis, and of principles."[22] When we ask this Yale law professor why he hates logic, his amazing answer is that he and other Consciousness III people have "been exposed to some rather bad examples of reason...."[23] This is a little like saying that since the grocery clerk added my bill wrong the other day, I'm never going to trust mathematics again. What if Reich's law students are exposed to bad logic in his classroom (as his book suggests they will)? Should their law practice be founded on a total contempt for the canons of reason?[24]

CONSCIOUSNESS III VALUES

In the second half of his book Reich presents a kind of Consciousness III Manifesto regarding ethics and value. He begins by saying, "The foundation of Consciousness III is liberation. ... The meaning of liberation is that the individual is free to build his own philosophy and values, his own life-style, and his own culture from a new beginning."[25] The demand for freedom is something everyone in the new generation insists on, but it is important to recognize the consequences of insisting on freedom without values and standards to guide its exercise. When you talk about freedom to build values, you are coming close to moral anarchy. But as we shall see in a moment, Reich doesn't practice what he preaches. Notice one more thing about this quotation. Earlier Reich made it clear that a person's values are a product of his social and economic condition. Now he talks about the *freedom* of people to create their own values. The two doctrines are obviously incompatible.

There are three basic commandments for Consciousness III people: (1) "Thou shalt not do violence to thyself." (2) "No one judges anyone else."[26] (3) "Be wholly honest with others, use no other person as a means." I only have time to comment on Reich's first commandment.

Consciousness III starts with self. In contrast to Consciousness II, which accepts society, the public interest, and institutions as the primary reality, III declares that the individual self is the only true reality. . . . The first commandment is: thou shalt not do violence to thyself. It is a crime to allow oneself to become an instrumental being, a projectile designed to accomplish some extrinsic end, a part of an organization or a machine. One must live completely at each moment, not with the frenzied 'nowness' of advertising, but with the utter wholeness that Heidegger expresses. The commandment is: be true to oneself.

To start from self does not mean to be selfish. It means to start from premises based on human life and the rest of nature, rather than premises that are the artificial products of the Corporate State, such as power or status. It is not an 'ego trip' but a radical subjectivity *designed* to find genuine values [my emphasis] *in a world whose official values are false and distorted.*[27]

It would be helpful if we knew what Reich means by the false values of the Corporate State and the genuine values he proposes to find. The phrase "discover genuine values" implies that there are objective values which the individual *does not* create. The phrase "false values" implies again that there are true values which serve as standards which judge human actions and decisions. Neither of these implications is consistent with Reich's epistemology nor with his earlier claim that Consciousness III believes the individual should be free to build his own values from a new beginning. I hate to sound repetitious, but repetition is hard to avoid when people insist on repeating the same errors. If a person's values are determined by economic and material conditions, then no one, including Reich, is free to choose or create any values. If no one should judge others, then Reich should stop judging the people in Consciousness II. If one is a radical subjectivist, then there are no false values to deny and no genuine values to discover. In fact, no values can have objective validity—including Reich's three commandments. You see, the only person who could consistently have written a book like *The Greening of America* would be a person who believes there are objective standards of right and wrong, standards which permit us to judge and evaluate the actions of individuals and societies. But then such a person would not belong to Consciousness III and thus would never have written the book in the first place. But let's give Reich one more chance.

All experience has value, all of it has something to teach, none of it is rejected because it fails to accord with some preexisting scheme of things. Of course this does not mean that the Consciousness III person will engage in actions that violate his basic values; he will never kill or rape to try the experience. But subject to these limits, he is open to trying new things; he does not judge or reject them in advance.[28]

Isn't it strange that in consecutive sentences Reich can say that all experience has value and some experience (rape and murder) does not have value. I'm glad Reich adds the second statement, but can't he see that if the second is true the first must be false? Since assertion and denial cancel each other out, a person who rejects logic ends up saying nothing. Furthermore, since any statement whatsoever follows from a contradiction, the person who utters a contradiction ends up saying everything.[29] Surely there are good grounds for concluding that *The Greening of America* is a confused melange of nonsense.

I am convinced that the arguments against Marcuse and Reich that I have presented are sound. The only thing left to decide is whether they are typical of the movement they represent. All I can say is that in comparison to others in the movement Marcuse and Reich are flaming rationalists. You can easily verify this through personal contact or through a study of the many books that either purport to speak for the movement[30] or provide an accurate description of segments of the counter culture.[31] The message that all in the counter culture should heed is this: If an individual is sincere in his search for the Real, he must not repudiate the Rational.

---

1. *Theodore Roszak observes that it is impossible to characterize the counter culture by producing a manifesto that all would approve. The movement lacks the discipline to produce a manifesto. Adherents of the counter culture are not clear about the Holy City they wish to reach. They have a better idea of what the Holy City, the New Jerusalem, is not like. See Roszak's* The Making of a Counter Culture *(Garden City, New York: Doubleday, 1969), p. 49. Kenneth Keniston reports that actual studies of young radicals reveal an almost total absence of "formal statements of rationalized philosophy, articulated interpretations of history and political life, and concrete visions of political objectives. . . ."* The Young Radicals *(New York: Harcourt, Brace and World, 1968), p. 28.*

2. *As a matter of fact, Reich utilizes Marcuse's critique throughout his book.*

3. *Aristotle's argument can be put in the form of a dilemma: If the opponent of logic says anything significant, then he must make use of the very law he is trying to refute, and if he says nothing, then we need not worry about his opinions since he fails to make them known. Either the opponent of logic says something significant or he does not. Therefore, he either makes use of the very law he is attempting to refute (thereby acknowledging the absurdity of his task), or else we need not worry about his opinions. This important argument is too complex to spell out in more*

detail here. The interested reader can consult The Philosophy of Gordon Clark, *ed. Ronald Nash (Philadelphia: Presbyterian and Reformed Publishing Co., 1968), pp. 126-39.*

4. *Aristotle,* Metaphysics, *1008b.*

5. *The link between ontology and epistemology, between the rational God and his creation, is discussed in my book* The Light of the Mind: St. Augustine's Theory of Knowledge *(Lexington: University of Kentucky Press, 1969).*

6. *Marcuse,* An Essay on Liberation *(Boston: Beacon Press, 1969), p. 11.*

7. *Marcuse puts it this way: "Men must come to . . . find their way from false to true consciousness, from their immediate to their real interest. They can do so only if they live in need of changing their way of life, of denying the positive, of refusing. It is precisely this need which the established society manages to repress to the degree to which it is capable of 'delivering the goods' on an increasingly large scale, and using the scientific conquest of nature for the scientific conquest of man" (*An Essay on Liberation, *pp. xiii-xiv). Later in the same book, he writes, "If and when men and women act and think free from [their identification with their false fathers] . . . they will have broken the chain which linked the fathers and the sons from generation to generation." The causes that have turned human history into a history of domination and servitude are economic and political. But since these causes "have shaped the very instincts and needs of men, no economic and political changes will bring this historical continuum to a stop unless they are carried through by men who are physiologically and psychologically able to experience things, and each other, outside the context of violence and exploitation" (pp. 24-25).*

8. *"In the last analysis, the question of what are true and false needs must be answered by the individuals themselves, but only in the last analysis; that is, if and when they are free to give their own answer. As long as they are kept incapable of being autonomous, as long as they are indoctrinated and manipulated (down to their very instincts), their answer to this question cannot be taken as their own. By the same token, however, no tribunal can justly arrogate to itself the right to decide which needs should be developed and satisfied. Any such tribunal is reprehensible, although our revulsion does not do away with the question: how can the people who have been the object of effective and productive domination by themselves create the conditions of freedom?" (*One Dimensional Man, *chap. 1). Indeed! This is just the question that Marcuse needs to and yet fails to answer.*

9. *One of three essays in the book* A Critique of Pure Tolerance *by Marcuse, R. P. Wolff and Barrington Moore, Jr. (Boston: Beacon Press, 1967).*

10. *Marcuse et al.,* Critique, *p. 109.*

11. *"For the true positive is the society of the future and therefore beyond definition and determination, while the existing positive is that which must be surmounted" (*Critique, *p. 87).*

12. *"Confronted with the total character of the achievements of advanced industrial society, critical theory is left without the rationale for transcending this society" (*Essay on Liberation, *p. xiv).*

13. *It is little wonder that at one stage of his thought Marcuse wondered wistfully if "perhaps an accident [might] alter the situation...." But as he continued, "Unless the recognition of what is being done and what is being prevented subverts the consciousness and the behaviour of man, not even a catastrophe will bring about the change" (*Essay on Liberation, *p. xv).*

14. *Marcuse,* One Dimensional Man *(Boston: Beacon Press, 1964), p. 137.*

15. *Charles Reich,* The Greening of America *(New York: Random House, 1970), p. 16.*

16. *Ibid., p. 4.*

17. *Ibid., p. 16.*

18. *Ibid., pp. 226-27.*

19. *Ibid., p. 16.*

20. *Ibid., p. 346.*

21. *Reich makes the first point on page 71. His support for the second is scattered through the book.*

22. *Reich, p. 257.*

23. *Ibid.*

24. *Two more quotations from* The Greening of America *are relevant. The first, from page 233, informs us that all is flux. "Because it accepts no imposed system, the basic stance of Consciousness III is one of openness to any and all experience. It is always in a state of becoming. It is just the opposite of Consciousness II, which tries to force all new experience into a pre-existing system, and to assimilate all new knowledge to principles already established. Although we can attempt to describe the specific content of Consciousness III at a given moment, its lasting essence is constant change, and constant growth of each individual."*

On page 257 Reich states, "At any rate, Consciousness III believes it essential to get free of what is now accepted as rational thought. It believes that 'reason tends to leave out too many factors and values—

especially those which cannot readily be put into words and cate-gories. . . . It believes that thought can be 'non-linear,' spontaneous, dis-connected. It thinks rational conversation [which apparently includes scholarly conferences as well as classroom lectures in modern law] has been overdone as a means of communication between people, and it has invented a new term, 'rapping,' for communication [sic] when it does take the form of words."

25. *Ibid., p. 225.*

26. *Ibid., p. 226. The context for this commandment reads as follows: "Consciousness III postulates the absolute worth of every human being—every self. . . . Instead of insisting that everyone be measured by given standards, the new generation values what is unique and different in each self. . . . No one judges anyone else. This is a second commandment. Consciousness III rejects the whole concept of excellence and comparative merit that is so central to Consciousness II. III refuses to evaluate people by general standards, it refuses to classify people, or analyze them."*

27. *Ibid., pp. 225-26.*

28. *Ibid., p. 257.*

29. *The logical statement form, $(p \cdot -p) \supset q$, is a tautology. In other words, any statement whatsoever follows from a contradiction. Any argument with inconsistent premises must be unsound because any set of incon-sistent premises would have to include at least one false premise. As Irving Copi points out, "Any and every conclusion follows logically from incon-sistent statements taken as premises. Inconsistent statements are not 'meaningless,' their trouble is just the opposite. They mean too much— they mean everything, in the sense of implying everything. And if every-thing is asserted, half of what is asserted is surely false, since every state-ment has a denial." Introduction to Logic, 3rd ed. (New York: Macmillan, 1968), pp. 267-68.*

30. *I refer, for example, to a book like* Voices from the Love Generation *or the poems of Allen Ginsberg or the books by Abbie Hoffman. One sample from Hoffman's* Woodstock Nation *(New York: Random House, 1969) should be sufficient: "When I appear in the Chicago courtroom, I want to be tried not because I support the National Liberation Front— which I do—but because I have long hair. Not because I support the Black Liberation Movement, but because I smoke dope. Not because I am against a capitalist system, but because I think property eats ----. Not because I believe in student power, but that the schools should be destroyed . . . not because I am trying to organize the working class, but because I think kids*

should kill their parents," p. 8.
31. *Examples would include such popular books as Tom Wolfe's* The
Electric Kool-Aid Acid Test *and more professional studies such as Lewis
Yablonsky's* The Hippie Trip.

Reason and Historical Reality
by Arthur F. Holmes

I
f the criticism stands which Professor Nash has presented, that Herbert Marcuse and Charles Reich contradict and therefore refute themselves by rejecting reason, then Marcuse and Reich have committed an unpardonable sin. They should be reminded of Hegel's quotation from Goethe's Mephistopheles (an authority in such matters): "Do but despise intellect and knowledge, the highest of all man's gifts, and thou hast surrendered thyself to the devil and to perdition art doomed."[1]

Of course neither perdition nor our criticism will silence the New Left for, as someone has observed, philosophical theories have a way of living long after their brains have supposedly been knocked out.[2] Yet their attitude to reason is sometimes obscured by an ambiguity in their meaning. I want to clarify their criticism of reason and to indicate why reason is important to a Christian view of things.

THE RULE OF REASON
The "rule of reason" is an idea that has dominated social philosophy since Greek and Roman times and was strongly reaffirmed by writers like John Locke, who helped lay the foundations of Western democracy. In brief, it regards the civil society as providing rational law and order to aid individuals in their pursuit of such rights as life and liberty. Analogous ideas emerged in the nineteenth century, not only in English utilitarianism but also in Hegelian and Marxist thought, where reason

finds its fullest expression in the state.

It is this idea of the rule of reason in our society which Marcuse and Reich now challenge. They agree that reason should guide us, analyzing existing conditions, identifying problems and determining what changes are needed in order to implement a more reasonable and equitable use of material and technological resources. But they complain that in practice reason no longer guides. Rather, modern society makes poverty, dehumanization and war seem necessary; political, industrial and economic technology have become unthinking monsters instead of useful tools for human ends. We neither act on our knowledge nor understand our problems nor act on our ideals. Reason no longer guides us to life and liberty. We have lost touch with those realities, and the rule of reason has become repressive.[3] It is time, they agree, for a change. Hence, while they seem on the surface to reject reason, they actually advocate refashioning reason in revolutionary style to put it back in touch with the realities of human life and liberty.

To understand this revolution we must recognize that Marcuse and Reich affirm a Marxist view of both reality and reason. They reject a certain view of reason because they reject a corresponding view of reality, not because they reject all correspondence between reason and reality. *What* correspondence they see, and what kind of reason corresponds to reality, depends on what they mean by reality. Their concern is with the material conditions of our existence, with the "realities" of modern society, with historical change and its socioeconomic causes, not with eternal moral laws or other ahistorical views of the real. If human reality is a historical process of social change, then reason must either fall into line or else fall behind and become irrelevant. They therefore indict certain kinds of reasoning for an irrelevance that represses the freedom of social change, and affirm instead another and more relevant kind of reasoning informed by imaginative and utopian goals, a reasoning that can provide the guidance and direction which technology and bureaucracy in both capitalist and socialist countries lack.

At the outset of *An Essay on Liberation*, Marcuse talks about updating the critical theory of society "to point beyond the existing state of affairs" to "a higher stage of development," to a social utopia that is now technologically possible but is blocked by a lack of practical reason. The function of reason is not speculation, and the function of theory is not understanding for its own sake. It is rather to change society. Reason, theory, philosophy—they are the tools of historical developments, not vice versa.

This conception of reality and of reason stands in stark contrast to the Greek view which Nash rightly claims they reject. The Greeks conceived of reason as speculation, as an intellectual vision, because they conceived of fully actualized reality as eternal and unchanging forms. But Plato had problems explaining history, and how its particulars participate in eternal forms. Is it any wonder, therefore, that Reich claims such reasoning is "out of touch with reality," defining reality as he does in terms of changing particulars?

What view of reason, then, corresponds to historical reality? In his early essay "The Concept of Essence,"[4] Marcuse opposes the "bourgeois" preoccupation with "absolutely certain, unconditioned, universally valid knowledge," for materialist (namely, Marxist) theory is concerned not with the unchanging essence of man but with the practical task of a rational reorganization of society towards a new potentiality. The essence of man is not static. He is still becoming. His is a socioeconomic becoming, with a history that is mediated in Hegelian fashion through the overcoming of opposites. The historical process is dialectical, and so must reason be. Dialectical logic points us from the bad current state of humanity to one in which goods are distributed according to need—real needs, not those created by the artificial structures of society. Rational man, in this sense of "rationally guided social existence," is *not yet* a reality. He is alienated from his reality. But he might now become real through the dialectical clash of opposites we are seeing in revolutionary confrontations.

In chapters five through seven of *One Dimensional Man,* Marcuse points out that dialectical logic is the logic of concrete, historical movements. In contrast, formal logic deals with universals and abstract possibilities. Formal logic is good at analyzing the implications of general statements, but far too limiting in a world of change where generalizations have limited life expectancy. In other words, like Hegel before him, Marcuse finds formal logic limited and trivial when it comes to the individual and the historical process. He also criticizes "technological reason" for making everything, including man and his labor, means rather than an end. This "instrumentalization" of man represses the freedom to imagine and realize new and qualitatively different forms of experience.

The problem with Marcuse's dialectic, to which Nash has rightly pointed, is its relativism—not about word usage, for such meanings often change—but about truth. His dialectic allows no unchanging moral principles and no unchanging truths that can transcend the effects of history. But dialectical logic does not altogether abandon basic logical principles such as the law of non-contradiction. When Marcuse calls our plastic society "obscene," he means "obscene," not "beautiful." When he refers to the Establishment, he means the Establishment, not the alienated non-Establishment. There are no contradictions here. Dialectical logic regards the principles of non-contradiction as trivial, however, when it comes to changing society.[5] The realities of social history, not abstract logical principles, are what ultimately count.

A NEW SENSIBILITY

In the revolutionary transformation of the rule of reason, the imagination is to guide reason, rather than letting it fall prey to repressive social forces. Marcuse calls for a "new sensibility" and Reich for a new "consciousness." They want reason to serve *real* human needs rather than those created and imposed on us by existing technology and institutions. That much sounds good, but "real" needs are seen to be simply the economic and emotional ones that are part of man's biological makeup, apart from any moral or religious or philosophical considerations.[6]

Apart from the materialistic presuppositions of such a definition of man's real nature, the call for a new sensibility heralds a kind of neo-Romanticism that is far more widespread in the counter culture than in the neo-Marxist segment alone. On all hands we hear Rousseau's "back to nature!" It finds expression in the experimental mood of the younger generation, in the hippie cop-out, in the return to Walden, in chemically induced fantasies, in overly optimistic hopes for man and his world. Logical and moral categories are reduced to the aesthetic. Everything is either "beautiful" or "obscene," whether ideas and arguments, people and their actions, or . . . you name it! It is here that I find the flight from reality most disconcerting, for by smothering self-critical rational analysis and careful moral evaluation under a blanket feeling, it condemns men, like little Linus, to learning the hard way—or perhaps not at all. It is a thoroughgoing relativism that prompts this post-Christian generation to fly from the sad realities of a bent world in search of a will-o'-the-wisp through heightened sensations and feelings, rather than seeking the meaning and purpose that are intrinsic to God's creation and are revealed and restored by the Divine Logos. Such a flight is symptomatic not only of the irrelevance of what may or may not be passé in modern society but also of man's much longer flight from God.

To fly from the sad realities of history is alien to Christianity. The Christian can no more return to Eden, whether at Walden or with Marcuse, than he can settle for the evils of society. For the Word of God stands in judgment on both the Establishment and the counter culture, on the one for its complacency and the other for its irrational unrealism about man's sin in God's creation.

But the Christian values this world as the creation of a purposeful, rational God. The Christian sees man as a rational being made in God's image. He values this world of men as the creation in which God incarnated himself, restoring life to men by reconciling men to himself. God is the Logos of all creation—its rational creator and its ultimate meaning.

There is, then, no dichotomy between the real and the rational, nor between being a person and being logical, nor between Christianity and culture. But there is a dichotomy between truth and error; for if there is a rational God, then, in the final analysis, truth is as unchanging as his perfect knowledge, and error is whatever falls short of God's truth. Man is not omniscient to be sure, but neither is truth relative. Rather it is given to man to know in part, often "through a glass darkly," but nevertheless to know. Man knows the truth very fragmentarily by most means, but he discovers its wholeness through what the biblical revelation declares concerning the Christ, "in whom are hid all the treasures of wisdom and knowledge."[7]

---

1. *Quoted by Hegel in his Preface to* The Philosophy of Right, *trans. T. M. Knox (New York: Oxford University Press, 1967), p. 6.*

2. *Leslie Stephen's observation, cited by Huntington Cairns in* Legal Philosophy from Plato to Hegel *(Baltimore: John Hopkins Press, 1949), p. 361. I insert the adverb "supposedly," for irrefutable refutations are very hard to come by in philosophy. On the subject of philosophical proofs, see John Passmore,* Philosophical Reasoning *(New York: Charles Scribner's Sons, 1961); also* The Monist, *48 (1964), iv; and* Revue Internationale de Philosophie, *8 (1954), 109-70.*

3. *See, for instance, chapter 1 of Herbert Marcuse,* An Essay on Liberation *(Boston: Beacon Press, 1969); and chapter 1 of Charles Reich,* The Greening of America *(New York: Random House, 1970).*

4. *First published in 1936 in Germany; translated in* Negations: Essays in Critical Theory *(Boston: Beacon Press, 1963), pp. 43-87.*

5. *Can the dialectical logician prove the validity of the dialectic? Can he know he's right? I think not. His own remarkably consistent use of the dialectic is insufficient evidence. The dialectical materialist accordingly appeals to empirical evidence for the dialectical movement of history, and this is his Achilles' heel. The evidence, as others have agreed, is incomplete; there is contrary evidence; his conclusion is itself an overgeneralized, re-*

pressive abstraction. See, for instance, Sidney Hook's Reason, Social Myth
and Democracy *(New York: Harper, 1966), part 2. First published 1940.*
6. *See chapter 2 of* An Essay on Liberation *and "Consciousness III" in*
The Greening of America.
7. *On the role of reason in society, see A. F. Holmes, "The Concept of
Natural Law,"* Christian Scholar's Review, *2 (1972), 195.*

The Counter Culture:
A Flight toward Reality?
by George I. Mavrodes

Professor Nash has called to our attention the work of Marcuse and Reich. In this brief comment I will say nothing about Marcuse because my own acquaintance with his writing is so superficial. I will devote the first part of my paper to Reich and to Nash's criticism of him. The second part of this paper embodies some tentative suggestions for our own approach to the counter culture.

Reich's immensely stimulating and provocative book, *The Greening of America,* has two distinct aspects. In part it is an attempt to describe, analyze and explain a prominent contemporary phenomenon—the counter culture. But the second aspect is an attempt to defend that phenomenon, especially to defend it in moral terms, and to promote it. One might, of course, have different attitudes toward these two aspects. We might, for example, be grateful to Reich for his description but reject his defense as immoral, irrational, etc. In Reich's book, however, the two aspects are extensively entangled, and it is not easy to separate them clearly. While I shall not attempt that project here, I will address myself primarily to Reich the advocate and to Nash's criticism of that advocacy.

REGARDING NASH'S CRITICISM
Nash's main criticism, I believe, is that Reich's position, and perhaps that of the counter culture generally, is profoundly irrational. And it is irrational, according to Nash, not merely in

the sense that it involves mistakes in reasoning, even very important mistakes in fundamental matters, but in the more profound sense that it involves an explicit rejection of reason, a denial of the canons of logic, a deliberate flouting even of the Law of Contradiction. This is Nash's charge. I believe that in general this charge is false, though no doubt there is some member of the counter culture against whom it may have some proper force. In particular, I shall argue that Reich does not himself reject reason, logic or the Law of Contradiction, nor does he advocate, approve or defend their rejection. More precisely, I hold that Reich does not reject logic or the Law of Contradiction in the sense in which these things are understood by Nash. And the mistakes and failures which may infect Reich's work are not due to any such rejection.

Nash has reminded us of Aristotle's argument for the Law of Contradiction. Aristotle's best-known formulation of that law is as follows: "It is impossible for anything at the same time to be and not to be."[1] With this in mind, let us look at a paragraph from Reich's first chapter, a paragraph which Nash cites (in a footnote) as evidence of Reich's rejection of logic, his relativism, etc. Here is the paragraph:

The logic and necessity of the new generation—and what they are so furiously opposed to—must be seen against a background of what has gone wrong in America. It must be understood in light of the betrayal and loss of the American dream, the rise of the Corporate State of the 1960's, and the way in which that State dominates, exploits, and ultimately destroys both nature and man. Its rationality must be measured against the insanity of existing "reason"—reason that makes impoverishment, dehumanization, and even war appear to be logical and necessary. Its logic must be read from the fact that Americans have lost control of the machinery of their society, and only new values and a new culture can restore control. Its emotions and spirit can be comprehended only by seeing contemporary America through the eyes of the new generation.[2]

Now, what is the meaning of this paragraph? It certainly

seems to speak of an old logic and a new logic, an old rationality and a new rationality. And the old is condemned here and
rejected, the new is hailed and accepted. Nash apparently believes that the old logic is the logic which consists of canons
such as the Law of Contradiction, and that must be what Reich
rejects. The new logic which Reich hails consists of—well, who
knows what? But if we actually try to apply this interpretation
to the paragraph under consideration it immediately rings false.
Reich seems plainly to reject the logicality of war and poverty.
On Nash's interpretation, this would mean that Reich, contrary
to Aristotle, is expressing in this passage the view that war and
poverty can both be and not be (in the same sense, at the same
time, etc.). But once one formulates this interpretation one sees
immediately that Reich here means nothing of the sort. He is
not speculating about the absurd possibility that war might
both be and not be. He has no quarrel here with Aristotle about
logic. The paragraph has an entirely different thrust.

A more modern formulation of the Law of Contradiction
might say that there is no proposition which is both true and
false, or that there is no proposition such that both it and its
negation are true. But is Reich claiming, contrary to these rules,
that there is some proposition about war which is both true and
false? Nothing in this paragraph, or elsewhere in the book, suggests to me that Reich believes any such nonsense as that. But
does not Reich here reject and condemn the old logic as insane?
Certainly he does. But does that not make it clear that he is
rejecting logic, at least the old logic of Aristotle, just as Nash
says? Certainly not. The fact is simply that Reich does not
mean by terms such as "logic" and "reason" what Nash means.
In particular, Reich does not mean the Law of Contradiction.

Let me reformulate Reich's paragraph without reference to
logic or reason. I think what it means is roughly this: "There is
a *Weltanschauung* [perhaps Reich would say a 'consciousness'],
that is, a complex of attitudes and beliefs and perhaps unreal-
ized assumptions which constitutes a way of thinking about the
world, such that if a person has that Weltanschauung, war and

poverty will probably seem to him to be desirable, or at least unavoidable, features of the best practical social arrangements. That Weltanschauung has been common in America, but it has in fact led to the loss of the American Dream. The new generation has a different Weltanschauung, and one can understand the new view only if one has some appreciation of how monstrous the old one is."

Something like this, I think, is the import of Reich's paragraph. It may be mistaken in some way or other, but it is compatible with anything which Aristotle, or perhaps Nash, has to say about logic. It is, in fact, not about logic at all. Consequently, it cannot be effectively criticized in the manner which Nash has chosen.

Since Reich is not talking about logic, I think it unfortunate that he uses the words "logic," "reason," etc. He uses these words as many college freshmen do (and many professors also), vaguely and ambiguously, with a multiplicity of meanings. When Reich speaks about "the logic of _____" I think he generally means something like the beliefs and attitudes which are a part of _____, along with the way in which they might plausibly be developed and the consequences to which they lead. On other occasions "logic," "rationality" and their cognates are sometimes used to mean science, sometimes plausibility, sometimes efficiency, sometimes the practice of basing decisions or actions on general principles, sometimes stability and predictability, and perhaps sometimes other things as well.[3] I am sorry about this ambiguity, for I think it detracts from the power of what Reich has to say. I much prefer the way that Nash uses these terms. It seems to me that he takes them in a more useful and precise sense. It is one thing, however, to say of Reich that he is ambiguous or imprecise or perhaps misleading, and quite another to say that he is profoundly irrational and that he is a rejector of reason. This latter has seemed to me to be Nash's criticism and I have tried to explain why I take this criticism to be mistaken. I think that Reich has something worthwhile to say to us.

THE VOICE OF GOD IN THE COUNTER CULTURE

I begin the second portion of this paper by reminding you of Paul's entry into Athens. Paul saw, so we read, that "the city was full of idols." Doubtless there was much in Greek religion that was foolish, much that was perverse, perhaps much that was wicked. But was there also in it some profound insight, some ground upon which a better edifice might be built? Apparently there was. There was already in Athens, even before Paul came there, the recognition that there was a god who was in some sense (though not in every sense) yet unknown in that place. It was a recognition insistent enough to be embodied in a public shrine. And Paul recognized that recognition and made it a part of his witness there to Jesus Christ.

I have said that there was this recognition already in Athens. But perhaps there is another way to put this. Perhaps we should say that God had already spoken in Athens, and his voice was not entirely unheeded there. And Paul, when he came, recognized the echo of the voice of God in the shrine to the "Unknown God," and he linked his part of the word of God to the word which was already there in Athens, and so it came about that through these two words "some men joined him and believed." I think this way of putting it is also correct.

Now, with Professor Nash, we have set foot in the city of the counter culture. As we walk through this city we shall doubtless find much that is silly, much that is perverse and wicked, perhaps even much that is irrational. Shall we also find in it some insight, some word that God has already spoken in this city and which has not yet been lost? Is there something here upon which the Christian may hope to build?

The answer which we give will depend in part on what we see in the counter culture, but it will depend also in part on our own theological understanding. That the God who made heaven and earth might be in some sense unknown in Athens fit in with Paul's own theological views. Hence he could recognize and accept this element when he found it expressed in an Athenian shrine. What I shall now propose, in a somewhat tentative way, depends in like manner on a theological view.

It seems to me that one characteristic theme of the counter culture is a hunger for experience, or, to put it in terms of our theme here, a hunger for contact with what is real, perhaps even for a collision with the real. And it seems to me that this hunger has at least two major elements, two "moments," each of which can be specified in part by contrast to something common in the "straight" culture. Let me sketch these moments as I see them now.

On the one hand there is an insistence, I think, on the *full* range of human experience, a demand that experience not be limited, sanitized, cut short. And this is often felt as a reaction to the pervasive abridgement and control of experience in the modern world. Perhaps we can develop this a little. No doubt we are here all wearing our shoes, and we have worn them all day. To a person who wears shoes the surfaces on which he walks feel much the same—not exactly the same, it is true, but nearly so. To the person who goes barefoot, however, the hot pavement, the gravel border, the fresh-cut lawn, the polished tile floor, the luxurious carpet are all very different. He apprehends their distinctiveness through his feet. That person—the barefoot hippie—has had a certain contact with reality today which we here have not had. And he has noticed, perhaps, that not only our shoes but a great part of our technology has the effect, sometimes intentional and sometimes not, of insulating us from the possibility of that sort of contact with reality. And so he casts about for a life style which will again open those channels.

But perhaps this is not the most important sort of example. In *The Making of a Counter Culture* Theodore Roszak quotes at length from two scientific reports. One deals with a possibly fatal neurological experiment performed on a feeble-minded woman, the other with an experiment involving the destruction of a rabbit's eye by Lewisite gas. The reports are technical, detailed, dispassionate, "antiseptic." There is no hint in them that the observer saw in these events any different sort of significance than if he had observed, say, a cube of sugar dissolving in a glass of water. Of both of these reports Roszak comments, "It is impossible to focus on the fact that the event is happening before a human observer."[4]

Perhaps we can put it this way. Either these reports do, or they do not, accurately represent the experiences of the experimenters who wrote them. If they do accurately represent that experience, then each report is an appalling comment on the experimenter himself. It indicates that he is almost totally blind to the world about him, insensitive even to those situations which he himself contrives and controls. He is a man without windows on the world, reduced to peering through a single tiny peephole, cut off from reality except at a single point. Whatever it is that has maimed him in this way, we must shun it as we would flee the plague. Perhaps we must set a mark upon such a man and make him cry "unclean, unclean" lest we too should be infected.

On the other hand, perhaps the reports are not accurate representations of the experimenter's experience. But in that case they are lies, or something like lies. They misrepresent and distort; they do not "tell it like it is." And they are dangerous because they may really make us believe, if we read enough of them, that this is all there is, or at least all that matters, in such situations. These lies may make us blind even if those who wrote them could see.

One feels, of course, like rejecting this dichotomy by saying that of course the experimenters are sensitive to more than appears in their reports. But in undertaking these experiments they were following out very specialized and narrow interests in questions of neurology and physiology. From their experience, then, they have abstracted and reported only those elements which bear directly upon those narrow interests. The critic, however, cries out that there are other interests, broader or deeper than these. In fact, he cries, the question of "cortical localization" (the problem being investigated in the experiment on the feeble-minded woman) cannot be a legitimate or viable interest at all unless it is embedded in some more profound human concern which gives it a real significance. But where are the recognition of that concern and the openness to the experiences which are relevant to it? Do we not see all around us the very opposite? Do we not even have a technical philosophy which claims to be empiricist but which assumes that the only real experience is that which is acceptable to the referees of the standard scientific journal? But the counter-cultural man often suspects now that there is more to reality than is to be grasped by these circumscribed and officially approved methods—perhaps much more. He wants to open himself on every side. Perhaps he sheds more than his shoes.

This hunger for a *fullness* of experience, then, for contact with the real on every side and in every way, is one of the major moments in the counter culture's emphasis upon experience.

The second moment I will mention more briefly. It is the demand that the experience be firsthand, not merely someone else's which is preserved in an account. The counter-cultural man is characteristically not satisfied by reading of the strange or exciting things which happened to someone who took drugs. He wants to try it for himself. He is not content to hear lectures on the dynamics of encounter groups. He must enter such a group himself. He must in his own person listen to electronic music or perform Yoga exercises. Whatever these things have to say he wants to hear directly and in his own being. He rejects, that is, what I have sometimes called the "Philosopher's Fallacy," the mistake of thinking that everything can be done by words. He may be an avid reader, but he is not much inclined to think that books are a substitute for living.

Now, perhaps I have idealized this theme and these aspects of it. But not very much, I think. No doubt in this, as in other cultural phenomena, elements of very different worth are mixed. But even in such things as the pervasive experimentation with sex and with drugs, it seems clear that there is more than a hedonic drive at work. These things are often, perhaps even characteristically, taken as *ways of knowledge,* as occasions in which one is open to something deep, and out of which there might come a new and life-changing understanding. And despite the aberrations and sins to which it may lead, despite the idols with which it may fill the city of the counter culture, I consider this hunger for contact with the real to be a very hopeful element. It seems to me that perhaps it is the modern analogue of that Athenian altar.

I say this, of course, because of a certain theological view. It seems to me that the concept of revelation is the most important epistemological notion in Christianity. Central to the Christian way of thinking about our knowledge of God is the idea that God comes to find man, that he reveals himself, that it is God who speaks. The Bible seems to me full of this notion from end to end. But now we see a whole cultural movement turning away from a stereotyped, controlled, abridged pattern of life toward a greater openness to experience, a greater readiness to risk what seems familiar and safe and to step into what may be unknown, mysterious, even fraught with danger. Here are not a few people but a substantial segment of our society recognizing that the "approved" life style of the contemporary world, its cognitive and noncognitive aspects alike, has not been very conducive to discovering what is the point of living, what the world really is all about. Here are people, a whole new culture growing up among us, who are saying openly that they suspect there must be more to life than has met the common, "straight," twentieth-century eye, and they are out to find it—people who seem to have discovered anew the hunger for the full depth of reality in their own experience. I find myself asking, then, whether the Spirit of God may not be in this, whether God may not be preparing to speak to men more widely than we have been expecting and perhaps in ways that we have not foreseen. Perhaps it is only a conjecture, but I find it not without persuasiveness. How close it is to being true I suppose we shall learn in time.

If this conjecture strikes you with some plausibility also, then I invite your attention to a last question. If the counter culture's emphasis on personal experience is the analogue of the Athenian's recognition of the unknown god, then what is the modern analogue of Paul's address on the Areopagus? What is to be our part (if, indeed, we are to have a part) in God's speech to the new world which is coming into being? The person who is already a Christian—what must he do when he meets a man who is in flight, but whose flight seems to be more a groping for reality than a retreat from it?

---

1. *Aristotle*, Metaphysics, *Book IV, chapter 4, 1006a, 2-4.*

2. *Charles A. Reich*, The Greening of America *(New York: Random House, 1970), pp. 2-3. In this paper, page references are to the Bantam Books (paperback) edition.*

3. *These uses occur throughout Reich's book. See, for example, pp. 94, 95, 103, 106, 139, 163, 171, 172, 176, 229, 258, 381.*

4. *Theodore Roszak*, The Making of a Counter Culture *(Garden City: Doubleday, 1969), pp. 275-78. This page reference is to the Anchor Books (paperback) edition.*

IV

Identity & Vocation

The Christian View of Work
by John Scanzoni

A verse from an American folk song written in Auburn, Alabama, around 1915 goes:

Captain, Captain, Captain, give me my time
Tired of workin' in damned ol' mine
Captain, Captain, can't you see
This pick and shovel is killin' me.

From a sign beneath a clock in a sixth-grade classroom in New York in 1930, the following was taken:

Work
Thank God for the Might of It!
The Glory, the Strength,
The Delight of It!

And here are three "noninspirational mottoes" seen in business offices in recent years:

I May Look Busy, but I'm Only Confused.
Your Call Has Climaxed an Already Dull Day.
Time Is Valuable — Why Waste It Working?

These noninspirational mottoes edge us as well as anything into a discussion of identity, vocations and "the flight from reality."[1] The lackluster image of work which they conjure up triggers the familiar question: "Is America becoming a leisure-oriented or consumer-oriented society characterized by the decline of the 'Protestant Ethic,' a general withdrawal from work, and an intensified search for substitute leisure commitments?"[2]

Even more current is the behavior of some college students,

who reject not just the traditional work ethic but also the basic values of achievement and success which underlie them, in favor of communal living and other life-style experiments. Does their behavior signal the wave of the future, in which work as we now know it will not merely be tolerated but will be discarded in favor of something "better"—something these young people consider to be reality? For one of their complaints against predominant vocational patterns is that they are unreal, meaningless and oppressive. They are unreal and meaningless because, as these students ask, a person works hard for what? Only to die, the same as the person who didn't work at all. These young people also allege that present work patterns are oppressive because they do not permit *self-actualization,* the total fulfillment of one's own unique personality. Work within the setting of the modern bureaucratic organization is seen as a barrier toward the discovery of true identity, of "Who I Am."

On the other hand, their elders respond to their complaints by asserting that they have not proposed any realistic alternatives to the present situation—that their attempts to escape the old unrealities may simply be an escape into the fanciful, utopian and equally unreal. The purpose of this paper, therefore, is to try to set forth a Christian perspective on these kinds of issues. Specifically, what is a Christian view of work in modern society? How is such a view linked to personal identity? And how is such a view of vocation and identity part of the larger "search for reality"?

HISTORICAL PERSPECTIVE

To put the current question in historical perspective, we need to go back to the beginning. In verses 27 and 28 of the first chapter of Genesis, we are told that God created male and female in his own image and that he commissioned them to subdue the earth and have dominion over it. Here we have an elemental statement of the Judeo-Christian view of work. God ordained that work should be a meaningful activity for both man and woman, and God did this *before* the Fall, before sin and death were part of the human condition.

Before the Fall, we read of Adam doing work in joyous obedience to God, essentially as a means to explore both his own mind and God's creation. For example, the writer of Genesis says that it was man, not God, who named the birds and the animals. We read that God brought the creatures to man and waited to find out what label man would give to them. And whatever label man gave, that label remained; God did not interfere. In addition to this mental task—this labor of the intellect—man was also given manual labor. Genesis 2:15 tells us that he was put in the Garden of Eden "to till it and keep it."

To me, this narrative suggests that work in its pristine form, as God intended it, is the exercise of God-given talents to create ideas and objects. Work is a blend of obedience to God and the full freedom to be as creative, as expansive and as uniquely individualistic as possible.

We also read that God rested from his work. His work of what? His work of creation. Creativity and work were, for God, synonymous. God made man in his own image. Man, too, therefore, is to create through his own work. Before the Fall, vocation and creativity were synonymous for man as well as for God.

But after the Fall, work took on a dimension which had not been present before. Work became a necessity to stave off death—at least temporarily. We may speculate that before the Fall man may have had abundant time and mental alertness to engage, for example, in primitive horticultural explorations. Afterward, for the masses of Earth's people, work meant wandering about gathering fish and game where they could or else searching for grazing lands for their flocks. And, for thousands of years, work became synonymous with grinding labor, with eking out a bare existence from the unyielding soil, completely at the mercy of insects, plant disease, drought, flood and so on.

It is no wonder, therefore, that "to the ancient Greeks, whose economy was slave based, work was a curse. According to Homer, the gods hated mankind and out of spite condemned men to labor. Although Greek thinkers conceded that agriculture might be tolerable for a citizen...they deplored the mechanical arts as brutalizing the mind. In general, the Greeks, like the Romans...saw work as a painful, humiliating necessity."[3]

In the Old Testament, however, as well as in rabbinical literature, we find the idea conveyed that honest toil, no matter how lowly in prestige, is honorable and pleasing to God. It is idleness and dishonorable work that are deemed offensive.

The New Testament continues these Old Testament themes, but both Christ and the writers of the epistles make explicit something that seems less explicit for the ancient Hebrews. And that is, that, since some people work harder or are more clever than others, or since some have better fortune than others with uncontrollable factors like weather, some have more wealth or gain than others. We are, therefore, repeatedly warned that when we seek wealth we run the grave risk of covetousness, which is idolatry, which means that mammon replaces Christ as the center of our being. The early church Fathers, conscious of the spiritual dangers of acquisitiveness and inheriting the Greco-Roman disdain for toil, conveyed the idea to their people that "work is best which least fills men with thought of profit and loss, which least distracts man from God."[4] Until the Reformation, the church maintained a strict dichotomy "between religious piety, expressed in meditation and prayer, and worldly activity, expressed in labor."[5]

The Reformers revived the idea that all honest work is honorable and pleasing to God, regardless of whether it is manual or nonmanual labor. However, subsequent to the first generation of reformers, the idea grew up within the church that economic success was a sign of God's blessing and favor.[6] John Wesley is quoted as saying that "religion must necessarily produce both industry and frugality, and these cannot but produce riches."[7] The so-called Protestant Ethic, along with purely humanist philosophies, began, in a context of burgeoning business and industrial opportunity, to create the notion that the "good," the "respectable," the "worthy" man is the man who is a good provider, who is economically well-off or successful. "He has God on his side," it was thought.

Social psychologists agree that identity, or self-concept, is largely the product of what the person thinks others think of him. If, for example, I think that others think I am unworthy, I am likely to think I am indeed unworthy. If I think, on the other hand, that others think I am worthy, I am also likely to think I am worthy. Consequently, for the last few centuries, given the Protestant Ethic and its grounding of male self-concept in material acquisition, the identity of most males in Western society has been based on their "economic success." The money that they earn has been translated into a display of visible consumption symbols by which others judge them as more or less worthy.

PRESENT PROSPECTS

And that brings us to the present, for it is exactly the dependence of identity on work and success that some young people are beginning to question. Moreover, their misgivings about material success provide an excellent opportunity for Christians to demonstrate the convergence that we have with them. For it has been a gross error for the Christian church to equate material or numerical success with God's blessing. It has been an error because it has riveted attention on the *outcomes* of work —the money, the power, the prestige—the things that, as Jesus said, the "Gentiles seek after." Instead, the Christian emphasis should be where the early Reformers saw it—on the sacred nature of the work itself. A useful distinction is between work as achieving, or process, and the outcomes of work in terms of material rewards and consumption symbols.[8] The Christian is in the world to work—to use his talents and gifts to explore and discover all he can about himself, about God and his creation, about others, and about the complex, modern world in which he lives. The emphasis is on the striving, on the *process* of achieving or working.

The results, the success, the outcomes, he leaves with God, who by no means guarantees success. In his sovereignty, he may permit what society would call failure or a dismal outcome. Those who have read Elisabeth Elliot's *No Graven Image* have seen this point made in terms of missions and other religious vocations. The same might be true of the Christian college student who, in spite of diligent efforts, flunks out, or the Christian businessman who, in spite of every reasonable attempt to do well, goes broke, or the Christian teacher or researcher who has given his best and still does not attain what his colleagues consider success. The Christian works chiefly for God and to please God, leaving the result—whether "good" or "ill"—in God's sovereign control.

Dietrich Bonhoeffer observed,

In a world where success is the measure and justification of all things, the figure of Him who was sentenced and crucified remains a stranger and is at best the object of pity. The world will allow itself to be subdued only by success. It is not ideas or opinions which decide, but deeds. Success alone justifies wrongs done . . . with a frankness and offhandedness which no other earthly power could permit itself, history appeals in its own cause to the dictum that the end justifies the means. . . . The figure of the Crucified invalidates all thought which takes success as a standard.[9]

This perspective immediately shifts the main focus of the Christian's identity from other people, who are constantly judging his success, to God, who instead judges his efforts, his faithfulness. Where before he may have been continually anxious about whether he was successful enough to earn the approval of others, he now sees that kind of outcome as peripheral. The display of material symbols to impress others thus becomes far less significant than the striving to please God through diligent work efforts. It is precisely at that point that the Christian message of vocation and identity can speak to the young person who questions occupational success and material display as a source of identity but is uncertain of any viable alternatives.

Incidentally, it is important to note that all available evidence indicates that only a tiny handful of students have completely rejected the whole package of work, achievement, success, material display, etc., and flown totally from reality into the hard-drug scene.[10] The vast bulk of students, plus the more than half of all youth who never attend college, fully expect to participate actively in the labor force, though they may do so in spite of deep misgivings about the worthwhileness of it all. It is these persons, as well as youth disillusioned with the drug scene, who could be shown that the resurrection and life of Christ give meaning to work, that work does not need to be an absurd exercise in futility, that it does have implications for immortality and for eternity. These persons could also be shown that work can be creative and fulfilling (and thus less oppressive) as they move into those positions that permit optimum exercise of their particular gifts and talents. They can also learn that their identity need not depend on vacuous material display or elusive success goals, but rather can be based on the intrinsic and genuine satisfactions that come from performing holy work for God, using the sacred gifts he has given. That is reality.

SOME SPECIFIC ISSUES

There are several specific questions which emerge from the foregoing discussion. One issue has to do with the significance of work per se as the United States moves into what has been termed a "post-industrial" society.[11] But post-industrial can be a misleading term unless we follow its original definition, namely, that on a solid base of advanced industrial development, the greatest expansion in a nation's economy comes in the service, educational and governmental sectors. The point is that many economists agree we can look forward to steady economic expansion throughout Western societies, the communist countries (including China, with its vast market of some three-quarters of a billion people) plus the whole Third World—Africa, Latin America, the Near and Far East. Berger and Berger, among others, have observed that the "greening of America" notion is more fancy than reality.[12] For the handful of upper middle-class white men who do tune out of the occupational scene completely, there are thousands of other young people—many from blue-collar homes—who are only too willing to take their places in the expanding world job market which seems to lie before us.

A second and related issue has to do with the alleged decline of the propensity to work; that is, we hear of the four-day work week or of the labor union which negotiates a thirty-four-hour week with six weeks of paid vacation, and we immediately assume that these are further evidences of the decline of work motivation in modern society. What we overlook, however, are studies which show what blue-collar workers actually do with the time provided by extended vacations or shortened work weeks: They "moonlight," or work at second jobs.[13] Their leisure is not spent in idleness but in self-imposed additional work.

Far more significant are trends toward ever-increasing automation which does away with many blue-collar jobs. It is the white-collar jobs—the professional, technical, managerial and service occupations—that promise to expand most rapidly in the future. To take one example, we now have the computer service man (a position unknown twenty years ago), complete with business suit and tie, who is on call twenty-four hours a day, much as the physician, to tend the ailing circuits of overheated computers. A recent major study shows that there is a growing minority of the male urban labor force which usually works fifty-five hours a week or more.[14] It is rarely the case that career-type vocations can be "turned off" after thirty-five or forty hours as a "job" often can. And since it is precisely these career-type vocations that promise to expand, while the number of blue-collar jobs decreases, we can expect a steady increase in the number and proportion of persons working more hours at more demanding occupations each year.

And that brings us to a third issue, that of minority groups (including in a very real sense, women) who have heretofore been excluded from a wide range of the most meaningful vocational opportunities. Careers may be a "drag" to some upper-middle-class white males, but to blacks, to blue-collar whites and to an increasing number of educated women, career opportunity is a strongly sought-for and coveted privilege. In the past, the church has unfortunately been in the forefront of limiting the opportunities of blacks and of women to exercise the full range of their gifts in the most creative ways possible. The church has done this by placing divine sanctions on invalid stereotypes: "Blacks are predestined to be slaves." "Blacks like to live and to go to school and church with their own kind." "Blacks are lazy, shiftless, and undependable." "Blacks should never supervise whites." Or "God ordained women to stay at home." "Women should only go into women's jobs, such as nursing, and never into surgery or into decision- or policy-making positions." "Women are not the equals of men." And so on, for both blacks and women.

The loss of these creative energies to the individuals concerned, to the Christian community and to society at large is immeasurable. On the road to reality, Christians must reverse their earlier obstructionism and take the lead in encouraging every youth, irrespective of sex, race or social class, to discover *all* the talents God has given him *or her,* and to feel absolutely free to enter *any* occupation where those talents can be most creatively exercised.

A fourth question pertains to religious vocations, or so-called full-time service. In spite of bland statements, such as "God needs Christian businessmen," there remains in Christian thought a hierarchy of occupations. Those occupations which presumably are directly concerned with "soul-winning" rank highest, followed by "secular" vocations that provide a "means to witness" while on the job. Adjectives such as *secular* or *full-time* should never be used to describe any Christian's vocation. *For him all work is equally sacred.* Translating the Bible or preaching or doing theology is no more sacred than mixing chemicals, nailing boards or doing psychology. In God's eyes, there is no difference at all in the temporal or eternal significance of these kinds of activities.

For a Christian, vocation is not primarily a means to anything extrinsic, whether it be material success or "souls" or whatever. It is primarily an intrinsic experience—coming to know oneself and God and the particular milieu in which one moves. The road to reality requires that we stop inflicting guilt and defensiveness on Christian young people who do not enter religious vocations. It is time that we emphasize that their vocation is equally holy service to God, as is any other vocation, *no matter what it is.* One vocation is as much a ministry, a sacred trust, as any other.

A final issue concerns the creative potential of many jobs in modern society. How innovative after all can the assembly-line worker or stenographer be? In response, we should note that for the great masses of people, modern society offers many opportunities for more creative, interesting and significant vocations than was or is possible in premodern settings. While some young people may romanticize the soil, there are readily available accounts of how quickly those who try communal farming discover how routine, ordinary and frustrating tilling the soil can be.[15]   Moreover, there may very well be many persons in frustrating jobs who are basically afraid to take the risk of moving out to vocations that are more challenging and thus more satisfying. A Christian concept of vocation, based on the creative exercise of God's gifts, might in some cases provide the motivation and courage to take a risk and to leave a safe but stultifying job for a more challenging vocation. Then, too, while a certain job may appear dreary to the outsider, the Christian in that vocation who is convinced that he is serving God, that he is doing holy work and thus using whatever gifts he has to the fullest extent possible—that Christian may be quite content, fulfilled and satisfied in his vocation.

In summary, I have argued that the prime characteristic of work as *creating* and thus *fulfilling* has often been blurred both in and out of the Christian community. The notion that work is a means to material success and to identity on that basis is being questioned by some young people as unreal, and they are searching for another kind of reality on which to base their identity. The Christian view of vocation as a creative exercise of gifts in holy service to God supplies meaning to work and a basis for identity that is real, in terms both temporal and eternal. The challenge to the Christian community is somehow to communicate this view of vocation as reality to *all* segments of our youth, whether disaffected middle-class white males or expectant blue-collar youth or suspicious blacks or newly-aspiring women.

---

1. *Harold L. Wilensky, "Work as a Social Problem," in* Social Problems: A Modern Approach, *ed. H. S. Becker (New York: John Wiley and Sons, Inc., 1966), pp. 117-66.*

2. *Ibid., p. 119.*

3. *Ibid., p. 120.*

4. *Ibid.*

5. *Ibid.*

6. *Max Weber,* The Protestant Ethic and the Spirit of Capitalism *(New York: Charles Scribner's Sons, 1958), pp. 110 ff. First published 1905.*

7. *Ibid., pp. 175-77.*

8. *See John Scanzoni,* The Black Family in Modern Society *(Boston: Allun and Bacon, 1971);* Sexual Bargaining: Power and Politics in American Marriage *(Englewood Cliffs, N.J.: Prentice-Hall, 1972);* Opportunity and the Family *(New York: The Free Press, 1970).*

9. *Quoted by Mary Bosanquet in* The Life and Death of Dietrich Bonhoeffer *(New York: Harper and Row, 1968), p. 225.*

10. *A popular account and documentation of these points is found in "End of the Youth Revolt,"* U.S. News and World Report, *August 9, 1971, pp. 26-31.*

11. *Daniel Bell, "The Year 2000—The Trajectory of an Idea,"* Daedalus, *96, No. 3 (Summer 1967), 639-51.*

12. *Peter L. Berger and Brigette Berger, "The Blueing of America,"* The New Republic, *April 3, 1971, pp. 20-23.*

13. *Wilensky.*

14. *Ibid., p. 125.*
15. *Herbert A. Otto, ed.,* The Family in Search of a Future *(New York: Appleton-Century-Crofts, 1970).*

The Christian View of Work:
Some Implications
by V. Elving Anderson

The basic point by Professor Scanzoni is that one's daily work can be a barrier to self-actualization or an important means of self-understanding and fulfillment. From a Christian perspective, it is essential that daily work be seen as a vocation or "calling." This view has several important implications.

First, Christian faith can be expressed in the context of a job, not just in what happens after hours. There is a fundamental misunderstanding on the part of one who says that his job is serving God but he makes shoes to earn a living. Ian Barbour justly criticizes the view that a Christian geologist is one who finds oil on church property.

A similar problem can be seen in the rather abrupt awakening of social concern on our campuses. It was indeed true that many professors (although by no means all) worked in relative isolation, with little effort directed towards problems of the community or nation. Rather abruptly it became much more fashionable to assume an activist role, and for this I am grateful. The problem was that energies came to be directed along channels quite separate from one's training or background. Thus the area for activism and social concern tends to be isolated from the rest of one's professional life.

Let me add a personal illustration. I entered genetics a few years before the DNA model of Watson and Crick. At that time human genetics had relatively few implications of a social or ethical nature. Now the possibility of genetic intervention and control leads quite naturally to discussions of freedom and responsibility and views of the future and the nature of man. Such topics now seem quite appropriate for a science classroom, even in public schools with a pluralism of religious backgrounds. My work with genetic counseling now involves the possibility of prenatal detection of genetic anomalies and selective abortion, and I have had to reconsider the ethical issues surrounding the abortion question. Our research work at the University of Minnesota has centered on the genetics of human behavior because the area has great social implications (and appropriate methods of investigation are available).

Some comment may be desirable on the strategic role of research as a vocation, in whatever field. It is quite understandable why the counter culture is critical. Research can be trivial and can even be a way of evading decision and action. But efforts at activism can be misleading and harmful if they run ahead of research. The new consciousness stresses the need for contact with reality, but the universe of matter and energy (which is explored through research) is a basic aspect of reality. The research scientist can feel that he is experiencing reality through his work even though the contact may be more indirect than walking without shoes. The point here is another illustration of Professor Trueblood's emphasis on *and*. We cannot choose between research and activism, for both are required.

CHOOSING FROM VOCATIONAL OPTIONS
Second, general acceptance of a Christian view of vocation still does not resolve an individual's choice among the various options. Scanzoni suggests that such decisions should be based on the gifts God has given, but some further qualifications appear needed. Abilities are not merely there waiting to be discovered. The range of potential is conditioned by biological inheritance interacting with early environment, but actualization requires development through experience. Furthermore, vocational choice is a process that continues through one's

working career.

One suggestion for young people is to try a variety of modes of expression in order to develop and test a personal repertoire. In this view, "failure" is not a reason for discouragement but a source of information and guidance.

But what if I don't like my "given"? At what point do frustrated efforts at exploration yield to a spirit of acceptance of my uniqueness, including its limitations? Recent developments involving the legal rights of the human fetus have sharpened the issue. In an Illinois court an illegitimate child sought damages against his father. The court held that a legal wrong had been inflicted on the child at the time of its conception, but recognized the implications of allowing recovery of damages in such an action for "wrongful life": "What does disturb us is the nature of the new action and the related suits which would be encouraged. Encouragement would extend to all others born into the world under conditions they might regard as adverse. One might seek damages for being born of a certain color, another because of race; one for being born with a hereditary disease, another for inheriting unfortunate family characteristics; one for being born into a large and destitute family, another because a parent has an unsavory reputation."

A further complication is suggested by the theoretical possibilities of "reprogramming" behavior by genetic or environmental means. It will be much more difficult than some popular articles have assumed to modify genes toward specified behaviors. But if even modest change is eventually achieved, what will be the response of the individual who may learn that some aspect of his behavior resulted from parental choice? Is it better to curse God or to curse one's parents for real or fancied limitations?

I raise these points not as objections to Scanzoni's paper but as some issues to be considered as we continue to think about a Christian view of vocation.

A third implication of Scanzoni's view is that an understanding of vocation as self-actualization should lead to great public concern about unemployment and underemployment. I appreciate Scanzoni's emphasis here.

Recently it has become clear that unemployment is not restricted to the untrained. Recent shifts in research priorities have abolished jobs for many scientists and engineers. Discussions about the national manpower pool should not minimize our concern for these persons as individuals. Some suggestions for changing the system include (1) the modification of requirements for jobs, (2) better prediction and feedback control to match training with future jobs, (3) education for the change that must be expected in an individual's lifetime, and (4) more effective means for retraining. What contributions can come from Christian insights and institutions?

Aside from such sudden shifts in job opportunities, the factors leading to unemployment are known to be complex. Alcoholism, petty thievery, emotional disorders, imprisonment and other problems interact and reinforce each other. Social services often are not readily available to those who need them.

Richard Herrnstein has recently suggested (*Atlantic,* September 1971) that the problem of unemployment will become even more acute in the future. After a clear discussion of intelligence testing, he outlined a syllogism for a society built around human inequalities.

1. If differences in mental abilities are inherited, and
2. If success requires those abilities, and
3. If earnings and prestige depend on success,
4. Then social standing (which reflects earnings and prestige) will be based to some extent on inherited differences among people.

One of the implications of this syllogism is that "as technology advances, the tendency to be unemployed may run in the genes of a family about as certainly as bad teeth do now. . . . As the wealth and complexity of human society grow, there will be precipitated out of the mass of humanity a low-capacity (intellectual and otherwise) residue that may be unable to master the common occupations, cannot compete for success and achievement, and are most likely to be born to parents who have similarly failed." The resulting stratification would not be as rigid as this discussion might suggest since genetic recombination would continue to provide considerable variability within each family. Nevertheless, there is enough validity to Herrnstein's picture to caution against a naive optimism about the future.

SUGGESTIONS FOR ACTION

How can a Christian perspective on self *and* community minister to these needs? What specific suggestions can we make for further study and action? I will list four:

1. Reference to the Protestant Ethic infers that a specific view of work has Protestant origin and continuing support. Whatever the historical background, I suspect that this phrase now represents a myth which should be exposed and rejected so that it is no longer considered an authentic Christian view.

2. All Souls Church in London sponsors a chaplain for some of the largest stores in the vicinity. What other patterns of ministry to workers have been used successfully?

3. Young people who are critical about our Establishment may be sensitive to possible new modes of vocation. Their collaboration should be sought.

4. Our evangelical colleges and seminaries are intended to aid in the penetration of society but the contact time with individual students is relatively brief. Alumni programs could extend and amplify the impact of these institutions by making continuing education their major function, particularly by encouraging a continuing examination of a Christian view of vocation.

Christian Perspectives
on Work and Leisure
by David O. Moberg

Basically I agree with Professor Scanzoni's thesis. The perversions of Christian values which have made the worship of mammon respectable and covetousness a virtue are at the core of numerous problems in our society. It is indeed unfortunate that even churches unwittingly fall into the trap of blessing anti-Christian values.

To a considerable extent, the youth protest movement is a reaction against the fallacies and hypocrisies of Christian people who have succumbed to such errors. As they reveal to us that the worship of mammon has replaced more important considerations and that a man's worth does not consist in the abundance of his possessions but in his relationships to God and man, they can help us awaken to our shortcomings and sins. As Scanzoni says, "Their misgivings about material success provide an excellent opportunity for Christians to demonstrate the convergence that we have with them." Numerous youths from evangelical families have rebelled against the conspicuous consumption evident when people go to church, trying to impress neighbors with their prosperity and presumably implying that they are better than people who dress less well. Let us rejoice whenever the Holy Spirit convicts us of sin, for only as we recognize our sinfulness will we be led to repent of it.

Similarly, I am entirely in sympathy with Scanzoni's emphasis upon the fact that all work of the Christian is sacred, although I would modify that statement. It holds true only when the vocation is fulfilled within a truly Christian context. Some occupations promote evil in society even if their personnel do not realize it; I am not sure that such work is truly sacred. Furthermore, Christian leisure is sacred, too.

WORK-LEISURE TRENDS

The trend toward "a steady increase in the number and proportion of persons working more hours at more demanding occupations each year" has been reversed since 1966.[1] This decrease may reflect only a general economic slowdown, but it may also represent a preference for leisure on the part of many people. In the May 1970 Current Population Survey, one-fifth of all employed wage and salary workers worked overtime. The majority of overtime workers are regularly on long work weeks. Only forty percent of overtime workers receive premium pay for overtime hours. White-collar workers are much less likely to receive premium pay than blue-collar workers, indicating a different set of motivations for their work activity.[2]

Multiple job holding ("moonlighting") seems to be increasing somewhat. Most moonlighters work at their second job over a relatively lengthy period of time. As of the May 1969 Current Population Survey, one in every twenty employed persons held a second job, working an average of thirteen hours on their secondary job during the survey week. Protective service workers (policemen, security guards, firemen, etc.) and farmers had the highest multiple job holding rates, but the highest reported rate of all was that of teachers below the college level, seventeen percent of whom had a second job. The rate for men was three times as high as that for women.[3]

In 1967 Professor Wilensky indicated that he was not convinced that the work week was getting shorter: "The skilled urban worker has now achieved the position of his 13th century counterpart, whose long workday, seasonally varied, was offset by many holidays, rest periods, and long vacations; annual hours of work now, as then, remain in the range of 1,900 to 2,500."[4]

At the same time, however, Wilensky indicated that modern populations remain busy but that some groups become busier while others are condemned to forced leisure. The upper social strata have lost out to lengthy work days and work weeks, so that even though their work lives are shorter and their vacations longer than those of the lower occupational strata, these men sometimes reach a startling lifetime total. Similarly, women frequently report averages of fifty to eighty hours a week in housework, child care and paid labor. "The 'leisure stricken' are not replacing the poverty stricken; the two are becoming one."[5] How to break this linkage of forced leisure with poverty (both during and prior to old age) is one of the major challenges of our society.

At the same time, it must be recognized that the percentage of one's life spent in work is decreasing because of the historical trend toward greater longevity, a longer education which defers entering the labor force and forced retirement rules. The work life of the average worker is longer now than it was several centuries ago, but life today is characterized by a growing proportion of leisure within the total life span.

PERSPECTIVES ON WORK AND LEISURE

I will not attempt to deal with conventional interpretations of work as a curse imposed upon man at the time of the Fall (Gen. 3). Scanzoni identifies this as making work a necessity to stave off death temporarily. Whether or not his exegesis is correct is a question I will leave to theologians.

Certainly there can be no question but that God's work in Genesis 1 and 2 represented creative activity; as Scanzoni says, "Creativity and work were, for God, synonymous." But I am not certain that all of the work of God is truly creative. To what extent is the sustaining work of God within the universe relatively routine and humdrum? A great deal of dull routine and dirty work is necessary among men today. To insist that all work be "creative" may simply turn people away from numerous necessary tasks that are literally dirty, having to do with the cleaning and removal of waste, or figuratively dirty, that is, laborious, lonely, dangerous or frightening.[6] We have tended to push our dirty jobs onto weak people and disfavored minority groups who lack power in the social structure. Perhaps it can be argued that all routine and dirty work can be done in a creative manner, but it seems to be extremely difficult to convince very many workers that such is the case.

Scanzoni suggests that Christians should have the faith to move out of safe but stultifying and frustrating jobs into vocations that are more challenging and thus more satisfying. Is this not saying, in effect, that such jobs should be pushed onto others? If so, how can this be reconciled with loving one's neighbor as one loves oneself?

In suggesting that the Christian should shift the main focus of his identity away from other people who judge by outcomes to God who judges instead by faithfulness, Scanzoni has, I suspect, overlooked an important intervening variable. Actually, human reference groups strongly affect our understanding of God's will. It is his will as interpreted by groups of which we are members or by theologians, preachers, and publications which we respect that dominates our practical experiences and thus forms our self-identity, even when we profess to be oriented to God alone.

Another false impression could be conveyed by the paragraph about leaving the results or outcomes of our endeavors with God. If we are good stewards, we will attempt to judge ourselves, to test all things, and then to hold fast what is good and to abstain from every appearance of evil. We will judge ourselves instead of judging others. This is evaluation, without which we cannot be good stewards of the resources and opportunities which God has given to us.

To view Christian vocation for its intrinsic values instead of instrumentally as a means to something extrinsic appeals to me theologically and philosophically, yet I wonder whether in fact that is entirely possible. If we speak of our Christian vocation as a means for glorifying God and serving our fellow men, can it be an intrinsic experience? Is it not instrumental?

Closely related to this is the question of guidance. If we over-accentuate the idea that every vocation is equally a holy service to God, no matter what it is, we may again face the problem of having apostles wait on tables (Acts 6:2). Vocational guidance in a Christian context evaluates personal ability in relationship to needs and opportunities in society. We must give due attention to the fact that not all people have the same gifts, hence not all are called to the same tasks (1 Cor. 12). Furthermore, I am not sure whether we can really know that "in God's eyes, there is no difference at all in the temporal or eternal significance of these kinds of activities." Is God's perspective that clearly revealed in the Scripture?

How much of our discrimination *against* minorities, whether blacks, women or others, really represents discrimination *for* ourselves? Much of the discrimination linked with labor unions, for example, represents protection of the security of working men and their sons.

Also, to what extent does the Old Testament, rather than the New, color our views? Is the male worth up to twice as much as the female (Lev. 27: 1-8) and thus worthy of higher pay, sanctioning the fact that men receive higher wages than women?

A most important topic related to Christian vocation is the problem of structural flaws in our society. The god of this world has all too often blinded our eyes, keeping Christians from recognizing our own involvement in customs which are degrading to other people and which are causing a great deal of suffering. We are so conformed to our social system that we engage in collective sin, thinking that conformity itself is righteousness. Our tendency to personalize praise and blame for human failings and social problems is a part of this difficulty. Because we are taught that he who will not work should not eat, we are tempted also to act as if his wife and his children should not eat. How to correct the problems of people who will to work but cannot, that is, who want work but cannot get it, so that neither they nor their families will suffer and so that the poverty cycle can be broken instead of perpetuated, is a major problem of our day. Our failure to provide work for the mentally disabled and people of only marginal competence is a part of this problem. Timothy Smith has proposed that the federal government guarantee work throughout life to every person who wants it and that we teach every child to grow up hoping for a job and assured that he will get one.[7] Some flaws may mar his proposal, but the basic principle is sound in terms of Christian values.

Scanzoni's intimation that the concept of Christian vocation serves as an opiate (making one content, fulfilled and satisfied) is in some respects analogous to Toynbee's idea that work is man's sovereign anesthetic: "It saves him from the solitariness that he fears—and his fear is well founded; for when a man is alone he is really alone least of all: He is then naked in the universe; he is face to face with God; and this confrontation is formidable. . . . Modern man . . . takes refuge in anesthetics, and most of all in the opiate of work, which keeps his thoughts away from contemplation by keeping his eyes fixed on the conveyor belt or on the drawing board."[8]

Work is a primary institution around which most other forms of social organization and activity are organized. It deserves a great deal more creative thought than has generally been given to it in our churches. Professor Scanzoni has contributed to that end.

---

1. Economic Report of the President to the Congress *(Washington, D.C.: U.S. Government Printing Office, 1971), pp. 232-33.*

2. *John Fenlon, "Recent Trends in Overtime Hours and Premium Pay,"* Monthly Labor Review, 94, No. 8 *(August 1971), 29-35.*

3. *Vera C. Perrella, "Moonlighters: Their Motivations and Characteristics,"* Monthly Labor Review, 93, No. 8 (August 1970), 57-64.

4. *Harold L. Wilensky, "Impact of Change on Work and Leisure,"* Monthly Labor Review, *90, No. 9 (September 1967), 21-22.*

5. *Ibid., p. 22.*

6. *Editorial, "Dirty Jobs,"* Minnesota Mental Health/Mental Retardation

Newsletter, *11, No. 3 (April 1971)*, 1.

7. *Timothy L. Smith, "Work and Human Worth,"* The Christian Century, *84, No. 35 (August 30, 1967)*, 1094-97.

8. *Arnold Toynbee, "Work, the Great Anesthetic,"* Milwaukee Journal, *August 6, 1971, part 1, p. 15 (Los Angeles Times/Washington Post Service; originally in* The London Observer*).*

V

Christianity
& the Counter Culture

Some Aspects of the Counter Culture
by John W. Snyder

After the spate of books, articles and addresses on the subject, my intention is merely to discuss certain selected aspects of the counter culture in its relationships with Christianity. I bring to the task the prejudices born of having been directly associated with that portion of the counter culture which has expressed itself as student dissent almost since its beginning. I have therewith confessed my belief that although the counter culture is by no means exclusively a phenomenon of higher education, it clearly has academic aspects; and to the extent that those academic aspects are a genuine and well-based cry for reform in the substance and techniques of education, I believe that they are still largely unanswered.

The counter culture is far from monolithic. It varies in time and place and mood and is most easily defined from the issues of the latest jamming. But it has certain common characteristics, sufficiently essential to make distinctions between it and related phenomena, such as beat and mod.

The first of these characteristics is its continuity with what went before it, the most recent being the Beat Generation, some of whose members are with us yet. Perhaps Allen Ginsberg is the best-known contemporary protagonist of the Beat. Behind the beats is a history of social criticism which goes back at least as far as Aristophanes' ribald puncturing of nearly everything both Athenian society and modern classicists regard as sacrosanct. Along a very different vein, but almost more in keeping with the SDS views on desanctification, were Jesus' far-from-gentle words to some among the crowds flocking out to hear and see him. "Generation of vipers," "whited sepulchres," "blind leaders of the blind" and "fools" are terms which, in their Near Eastern context, are fully as freighted as today's four-letter epigrams.

This long-standing pedigree of the counter culture is stressed because of the immediacy of nearly everything else to appear in these remarks. It is not correct to think of the counter culture (as Roszak seems to) as solely critical of technocracy.

Also like social criticism of much longer standing, and more general in nature, is the counter culture's choice of cultural forms for its manifestation. A culture-wide change is sought, rather than a partisan view within a dominant culture. This is because sensitivity is a problem of attitude, and attitudes are woven into the very fabric of culture. To this argument from the counter culture itself, I would add another motive: the use of cultural badges for identification purposes, about which I will say more later.

TECHNOLOGY THE VILLAIN

In recent years, technology has become the major target of all this criticism because of the changes in technology itself. Where once it came to the rescue of the Old Left, to the New Left it has become the villain. What follows is an economically unsophisticated, interpretive account of the arguments of dissent.

The massive and pervasive character of modern culture would appear to depend upon technology for its sustenance. This seems true for the production and distribution of necessities at the prices around which most of us have packed the remainder of our budgets. Given current levels of dependence upon transport and secondary distribution instead of local subsistence production, a sophisticated technology is needed to maintain prices that are feasible with regard to what people must pay for housing and access to work. The fact is, we do need the railroads, automation and all; we would be better off if they would work *better,* not at lower standards.

Thus established, dependence upon technology has, however, achieved more subtle forms in the following sequence: Price depends among other things upon quantity of production, which depends among other things upon the extent of the market, which depends among other things upon advertising, which depends among other things on the ability to persuade. So markets are managed in a process demanding sophisticated psychology, the use of media, restraint of access to other goods, manipulation of dealerships, etc. Who knows, at the end of such a sequence, whether the price of a quart of milk is "fair"? Probably it is true that the best way to tell is to look at the financial operating statement of the company and, failing that, to check its dividend record.

Much of this kind of technology depends upon the control of information. Brzezhinsky's *Technitronic Age* probably would have a wider impact upon the denizens of the counter culture if it were more widely read. One suspects that these new disestablishmentarians think that the technological aspect of their case is proven as things stand. Important to the control of information is incessant use of media. Noise has become an item of great technological concern in the theory of communication. Yet communication manufacturers have consciously pitched the media din at what they conceive to be just below the noise level, making it as insistent as possible without becoming self-cancelling. Secret records, Lucy, confidentiality, bugging, Bonanza, personnel forms, the need for gusto, quantitative social research, simulation, brighter toothpaste, media ratings, interviews, questionnaires, Mission Impossible, army files and the Internal Revenue Service have all made the information monster loom very real in the lives of many who would rather die than be part of the counter culture. Very probably, if more people were aware of how easy it is to know things about an individual that he does not know about himself through various quantitative analytical techniques, the voices of protest would be more shrill than they are now, as reported recently in *Playboy*. My point here is that the technology is ubiquitous.

Ubiquitous technology has taken what its critics allege to be a wrong turn, in fact, many wrong turns. Manipulation of taste for market management is only one of the ways in which it has strayed. Marcuse (*Negations,* 1968) wants us to understand that the problem is much deeper, that it is part of the ideological structure of technological society itself. One important way in which this is true is the insistence in modern society upon the *performance principle,* which demands peak performance in progress and production by all individuals under penalty of a full coterie of internalized guilt processes. A fundamental principle of the resulting society is the lean-and-hungry drive to do more, and to do it more cheaply and with ever widening application at whatever cost, to those who fail, to land and sky. Entirely gone is the principle of regard for and involvement with others (*eros* to Marcuse, who disdains any difference between this word and *agape*).

Symptomatic of technology's fundamental error in thought is the whole idea of optimization in foreign policy. *All* the world should be at peace; it can only be so if it adopts Western democracy; its failure to do so is a constant threat to those democracies by virtue of the domino theory (though other theories of spreading interaction will do as well), therefore *all* the world can be, and must be, policed. Since no one else is available for this laudable but generally misunderstood task, the United States must do it. The most recent result of this type of reasoning is perhaps the dollar crisis; other results can be read in *The Ugly American* or seen in the Bay of Pigs.

The information revolution, which we have already noted, constitutes another wrong turn. Beyond being a nuisance to some, it may even now be the ominous beginning of events leading to Asimov's *Caves of Steel* (if it goes well) or to *THX 1138* (if ill).

In summary, the counter culture's indictment of society includes a rejection of technology's insensitivity, a determination to employ and enjoy cultural badges to mark that rejection, and a repudiation of technology's massive character and wrong-headed nature. It also has its positive side—perhaps not the program the silent majority demands but at least one not entirely and constantly negative.

THE NEW MAN

Careful so far to avoid the primitive Christian crisis-conversion terminology, some seeking to speak for the counter culture reiterate Reich's theme of Consciousness III (*The Greening of America,* 1970) and announce the presence among us of the new man. I have found the idea echoing in very high places among scholars who seem charmingly unable to recall that both the Scranton Report and Reich previously discussed the notion. (For instance, see Robert N. Bellah, "Evil and the American Ethos," in Sanford and Comstock's *Sanctions for Evil,* 1971.)

The new man can be recognized by his cultural badges. These, however, are as rapidly being taken over by the Establishment as mod designers can sanitize them: hair, dress, undress. Not to be stopped with appearance alone, fads turn as well to vocabulary, drugs, attitudes about society, music and other things. Of these, even the counter culture seems in large part to be coming to the realization that drugs and some attitudes are counterproductive; the rest is being pre-empted. This presents a problem which literature probably first records by the pen of Homer: the deliberate use of culture for identification purposes when Odysseus was cast ashore among the Phaiacians. The process of badge-identification—pre-emption—new badge has been going on ever since.

Moreover, beneath a crust of hostility towards police and the drive to desanctify all in power, there is a set of attitudes belonging to Consciousness III which Reich perhaps best, if not with complete clarity, sets forth. Consciousness III *knows,* he says, government pronouncements for what they are (citing the Rockefeller visit to Latin America as an example of a governmentally joyful description of what was probably quite a nasty situation). Reich is too gentle to carry his description to its logical end: Consciousness III might well be intransigent in its rejection of anything said from power, from Washington or from a source over thirty. The new man has his values, however. They are affective, immediate, identifying, accepting, naturalistic and numinous, to mention a few characteristics.

Affective behavior (now big in education) is defined as that portion of intellection reserved for intuitive, appreciative, emotional behavior; those mental activities and their physically coordinated outcomes relating to aesthetics, empathy and, rather imprecisely, sensitivity.

Immediacy comes out in the directness of statement and impatience with forms of delay, such as deferred goals or channels of communication. Identity has become a cliché, the identity crisis. Beneath that is the relatively simply matter of defining oneself in terms of the differences and the similarities one notes between self and others. The specific difference in this regard with the counter culture is merely that identities are emotionally surcharged by noting similarities and differences in a group that has set itself apart from general society.

Acceptance of others is a much-touted principle, still highly selective in its application. Doing your own thing does not include cleaning up Telegraph Avenue; acceptance of others does not necessarily include doing the dishes in a commune. What it *does* do is consciously attempt to establish friendly relations with almost anybody but with common agreement that the Establishment generally just is not open to friendships. Implicit in this acceptance is Marcuse's *eros* in place of the performance principle.

Naturalism expresses itself in organic gardens, nature hikes, the aesthetic side of the concern over pollution, doing without brassieres and often without clothes. Reich's statement that no one in bell-bottom trousers can ever take himself seriously seems to miss the point on all this.

I have used the term *numinous* slightly out of phase with its dictionary equivalence to *spiritual* to stress the awe, the sense of nonmaterial experience, that surely can accompany things of the Spirit, but which also characterizes expressions of interest in occult matters as well. Among the numinous in this sense appears at times the notion of mystical awe with regard to sex. Stores market the paraphernalia of the occult; television and *Life* feature witchcraft and Satanism; books appear on the spread of transcendentalism. Some serious research on ESP and related phenomena aside, perhaps the most obvious characteristic of this kind of numinous interest or preoccupation, particularly when it is influenced by drugs, is its rejection of the normal canons of logic. Roszak describes this rejection of logic in its more sociological forms as one of the important ways in which the tyranny of technology can be overthrown. Because it has implications in several directions, one of his paragraphs is worth quoting:

In contrast to such selective skepticism (as Bultmann's), the wholesale skepticism of science shows up to brilliant advantage. Science is the infidel to all gods in behalf of none. Thus there is no way around the painful dilemma in which the religious traditions of the world have found themselves trapped over the past two centuries. Every culture that has invested its convictions in a temporal-physical mythology is doomed before the onslaught of the scientific unbeliever. Any village atheist who persists in saying "show me" is in the position to hold up to ransom an entire religious culture, with little expectation that it will be able to find the price demanded. It would be difficult to say whether this situation partakes more of farce or of tragedy. Only a few generations ago, Clarence Darrow, no more than a skillful courtroom lawyer armed with a Sunday supplement knowledge of Darwin, was able to make laughingstock of a Judeo-Christian mythology that had served to inspire the finest philosophical and artistic minds of our culture over hundreds of generations. Yet, under unrelenting skeptical pressure, what choice have those who cling to temporal-physical mythologies but to undertake strategic retreat, conceding ever more ground to secular, reductionist styles of thought. The line of retreat

falls back to interpretations of myth that are primarily ethical
. . . or aesthetic . . . or, in some unspecified fashion, symbolic.
Within the Christian tradition, this is a resort which is bound to
weaken and confuse, since Christianity has had a uniquely sig-
nificant commitment to the literal truth of its teachings. In-
deed, the sweeping secularization of Western society that has
come in the wake of scientific advance can be seen as a product
of Christianity's peculiar reliance on a precarious, dogmatic
literalism. Such a religious tradition need only prick its finger in
order to bleed to death. And if the hard-pressed believer does
turn to "symbolic" interpretations, even here the secular tem-
perament tends to sweep the field by asserting reductionist
psychological or sociological correlatives for the myth. The only
other defense, that of standing fast in behalf of the literal truth,
leads, as Kierkegaard recognized more than a century ago, to
the crucifixion of the intellect. (The Making of a Counter Culture, 1969, pp. 211 f.)

Perhaps this amounts to making a virtue of deviance when
applied to numinous inquiry into witchcraft as part of the myth
needed to purge mankind of the misdirection of technology. In
contrast to this deviance, Roszak appears clinically antiseptic to
the wanderer among the street people on a Friday evening,
recalling the days when sex was dirty and the air was clean.

WHAT THE COUNTER CULTURE IS NOT

A word about some of the things the counter culture is not. It is
not very widespread; its constant problem is the propagation of
its multitudinous views in order to widen the revolution. This is
not to suggest that it is insignificant but that an actual count of
hard core subculturists finds them highly transient, in the apparently deliberate attempt to appear numerous when needed at
one location or another.

They also are not very socially radical, beyond great attempts
to appear way-out in their use of cultural badges. Perhaps the
best illustration of this is the archconservatism that keeps extra
marital living together jealously monogamous. This tends to

confuse the edges of the counter culture, making its number and significance hard to descry. We are, therefore, required to make distinction between at least two major movements within the counter culture.

The first of these I have come to consider made up of highly conservative and constructive reformers who work mightily just outside the Establishment and whose long hair, shirtless perspiration and insistence upon first names are deliberate signals of belief that technology is desperately wrong, though wrong only in having shaken off its reins and roared on without rational direction. All who do not perceive this are the enemy; all who will attempt to work towards reforming the system are at least tolerated.

The second stream has been genuinely radical in the past but now is polarized into self-destructive anarchy on the one side and passive and often drugged resignation on the other. From this group came in the past the strategies of the Left which proved so successful at Columbia and against the Democratic National Convention in Chicago but which backfired at Kent State and now go begging—and which probably will surface again if the malaise of purpose, communication and technique continues unabated in higher education.

The conflict of viewpoint, between those who demand change and those for whom the best change now would be a return to the attitudes and student-faculty ratio of two decades ago, continues through communications which seem to pass each other in the night. The chief motivating force for confrontation is frustration borne of insensitivity and irrelevant information, say the expositors of unrest; nonsense, arrogance on the campus and slippage from decent standards of behavior and industry, say the still ensconced arbiters of faculty opinion and privilege. Unfortunately, both are right, a point which suggests itself as something to be considered in assessing the significance of what passes for radicalism in education.

The counter culture also is not terribly coherent in providing explanation of the feasibility of some of its apparently major tenets. A slight depression in everyone's living standards, we are told, would reduce to manageable terms the threat of pollution. The point is illustrated with organic gardens, disregard of liability, occasionally haphazard cleanliness, rejection of the Establishment's expensive standards of dress and convenience. We can congratulate ourselves that they are not yet running our trains or building our highways.

Consequently, it is the Establishment that grapples with fierce problems of nondemand economics in attempting to develop financially feasible transportation alternatives that would help clear Southern California's air. The serious observer wonders how to maintain adequate distribution of goods and services, how to control inflation without continued and even greater stress on productivity. Insects, we are told, continue to gain on man in the race for survival by virtue of their ability to generate immunity against changes and insecticides. Food production and distribution lag behind population; the Green Revolution creates more problems than it solves; nobody knows the long-range effects of solar storms through the atom-blasted hole in the Van Allen belts. These are problems which seem to demand greater, not lesser, applications of technology, an increased load on the performance principle Marcuse finds so basically unsound. A Malthusian martian, should he exist, might be forgiven for wondering if humanity does not have lemming-like safety valves which persuade the young to refuse to fight when war becomes self-destructive, to refuse families as immoral and threatening demands against a tottering ecological balance, to refuse participation in the technostructure they hold responsible for the browning of America. But who *will* solve problems of war, famine, overpopulation or pestilence? Technology may not, we strongly suspect; but Consciousness III seems even less reliable.

ONTO THE STREETS

The counter culture, with these problems of logical ambivalence, which it apparently seeks to smooth over by rejecting logic and other Establishment hang-ups, surely would never have left places like Greenwich Village and Sausalito for national prominence without the triggering mechanisms of the past decade and a half. Society has always functioned in spite of its "sanctions for evil." The threat of social damage long has authorized exploitation and repression. Mobilizing public opinion in irrational causes has often built the "superego in uniform," and has long relied upon group-think and dehumanization in processes aided and abetted by authoritarianism of conflict as well as the drive for wealth and status. So what's new? The triggering action of current conflict has occurred in three major areas, civil rights, war and pollution, and has brought the counter culture out of its ghettos and onto the streets and campuses.

Civil rights and poverty issues afford an appropriate arena for Marcuse's notion of *negations* regarding the ways in which progress can be self-defeating. Resources have been depleted and polluted, distribution is inadequate as shown simply by the poverty-plenty contradiction riding our cities and land. The causes of all this elude Marcuse, as they do most of us, myself included. Grappling with the problem, I prefer to put civil rights and poverty together, as I note that for a long time "civil rights" was thought to be a Southern issue; there, not in the North, came the early Supreme Court decision. Then came the discovery that Northern ghettos were as fierce, if not more so, and now *Ebony* is printing articles on the advantages of the South for blacks. It probably is a measure of the success of efforts to achieve civil rights that most of the conversation in and out of HEW and reverberating around the nation's campuses now concerns women's rights. One can discuss—and legislate—civil rights, but poverty is the real problem—poverty in all its forms of mind and body. The backwaters of Appalachia aside, the predominant problem is urban growth without adequate education, employment, housing, services and taxes.

Since populations never have formed a sheet distribution, but rather the lattice structure of centers of transport and production and their connecting arteries, the shift of people from country to city was never a trade-off. Economically, their previous rural subsistence was meaningless; economically, they flooded into the cities out of the blue and in unpredictable numbers, made the more explosive by the operation of social services, insecticides and detergents on birth and mortality rates. There they sought menial jobs in a sophisticated economy and became a fossilized labor market left only with their rising expectations. Lagging in pay, perquisites, time and conditions, and pushed out of work by the progressing sections of society, they became tyrannized by it.

So it might be fair to say that lack of understanding, inability and unwillingness to control private lives, snoring in the cigar smoke in city hall, all helped to produce the poverty problem, and poverty in turn greatly complicated civil rights. It is probably not fair to suggest exploitation except after the fact. And meanwhile the counter culture protests, joins and often serves in attempts to ameliorate, until driven out by frustration. The Establishment's record is lousy, too. Meanwhile, poverty, disadvantage and exploitation are there amid wealth. The association of these two provided one of the triggers.

Vietnam is another. One hears no arguments now on the streets about the war; one is either dove or neanderthal. The Calley trial, atrocity pictures, drugged veterans, POWs, disintegrating Vietnamese democracy—the list requires only the time to write. The war is there and it should not be. Because we had not the wit to avoid it, technology, seen as the military-industrial complex, is blamed. The more perceptive may mention that not engineers nor generals, but Harvard Junior Fellows got us into this war, and still more perceptive questioners wonder about Diem and Cardinal Cushing or Franco-American relations and Ho Chi Minh. Bernard Fall is dead but his *Last Thought on Vietnam* probably needs no sequel. Also dead are Eisenhower, de Gaulle, Cushing, two Kennedys—nearly all the protagonists whose reasons may once have been rational.

Those left to pick up the pieces must ponder the effectiveness of our foreign policy and its motivations. It's not a new thought at all with Alex Campbell (*Unbind Your Sons*, 1970) that America, like Rome, has found no alternative to treating nations as pawns in a giant game of dominoes. Again, perception depresses the question to other levels of noting the inevitability of satellite states for any large power and wondering who now plays dominoes in the Indian Ocean, perhaps while playing *March Slav*. And readers of *Fortune* and *Forbes* have known for years of industry's frantic efforts to diversify away from war materiel. However, the counter culture seems not to read *Fortune* or *Forbes,* except when searching for rhetorical ammunition.

But the question comes back: Do we in large measure create our own enemies and bobble into war? If we do, says the counter culture, it's the Establishment that does it. Widespread massive frustration made the war available as a trigger. Bobbing and weaving between the Bay of Pigs and My Lai on footing made slippery by spilled Pentagon papers, we do seem to be questioning our own military as never before. We are told to look higher up by a counter culture itself made possible by the fact that above the President stand the people of this land.

POLLUTION

Pollution is yet another trigger. Perhaps skinny dipping and organic gardens are not the answer, but few can deny that man is the Earth's disease. And perhaps nowhere is the counter culture's cry against the monolithic, massive insensitivity of technology so stridently heard. *Playboy* informs us pollution now is the number one issue with all the young—at least all surveyed by *Playboy*.

While many industries have cleaned up (the roster of their names can be taken from the advertising pages of the slick magazines), many have not. The Four Corners (of Utah, Arizona, Colorado and New Mexico) look like Anaconda and environs fifty years ago. Fifty years from now will Navajo land also be poisoned to the last blade of grass? One west coast city I know of would rather lengthen its sewer outfall line and bring cancer to more fish than contemplate recycling, despite a projected $117 million saving (according to the party *not* in power) over the next twenty-eight years. California's defeated gubernatorial candidate in the last election got free TV coverage by touring Los Angeles polluting factories, and they go right on. Whatever industry's reply, pollution triggers dissent because it is not stopping.

What of Christianity in all this? First, Christianity and the Establishment have always alternated between hostility and pre-emption. The current rash of Satanism reminds us coldly about the one whom the Bible calls "the prince of this world." Hence Christianity and success have always existed in a love/hate relationship. We love beauty and the pleasures of the soul while we worry to exercise the insights of the spirit. Stability is our stock in trade, and occasionally even wealth, but we are called to serve in the least position in unreciprocated charity.

Equity we support, and compassion, but we cry for law-and-order when mental and emotional starvlings senselessly riot. And after the peace of desolation settles over the burned buildings, what do we do when we have got our law and order? Responsibility and joy in good jobs well done we praise, constantly looking up—or we are supposed to—for the coming of another world.

This soul-rending ambivalence is a dangerous rite of passage for our young, most of whom we call to go through it without a whisper of help because our ambivalence sits so heavily on our own shoulders still. The truth is, Christianity was always a counter culture itself, its styles usually designed to set it apart like cultural badges. Subtly now, some young Christians pass from their fathers' counter culture badges of strait laces and no movies to the world's counter culture badges of long hair and loud music without ever going through the tinsel cocktail circuit our generation strove to avoid.

Other parallels spring to mind. From flannelgraph to sensitivity session, we have struggled to follow the biblical precept to love our neighbors cognitively and affectively. Naturalism may find its counterpart in spirituality. Unfortunately, along with the Protestant Ethic, this has been blamed for the Christian Establishment's ecological shortcomings in decrying yet another sanction for evil. Numinous, too, we can claim, as does C. S. Lewis, and mean by it an awed appreciation of mighty Providence.

I can maintain the intended ambivalence of this paper, I think, by stressing joy. We can pity the sham and shallow protestations of joy by Consciousness III from the lofty view of those whose joy is in the Lord. Can't we?

Also, we too are not very wide-spread. Except for the Jesus freaks, we are not very socially or spiritually radical, nor overly coherent to the world with our answers to problems. Yet we are a counter culture of longer pedigree than beat, Bohemian or hip. If we cannot salt the earth of technitronic machinery and counter culture alike, we will go with them into the caves of steel. That is, unless we are rescued.

The Secular Prophets
and the Christian Faith
by Clark H. Pinnock

There are three important issues which Professor Snyder has lightly touched upon which call for clearer and more emphatic statement. They are three lessons which, I believe, God wants to teach us through the counter culture.

The first point which comes through loud and clear is the conviction that material affluence divorced from human and spiritual values is empty and meaningless. The parents of these kids came through some hard times, have tasted the cake and are greedy for it. But the kids have had so much cake they are sick of it. The price Daddy paid for his affluence was too high— spiritual poverty, mindless technology, social manipulation. To attain this material security, Daddy has had to discharge his parental duties financially rather than paternally, and the family has suffered as a result.

Looking back on their homes, the kids find little to inspire them toward deep and loving human relationships. They do not want to go that route. Why should they? Why should we? We can see their ideal in the SDS Port Huron Statement: "We regard *men* as infinitely precious and possessed of unfulfilled capacities for reason, freedom and love . . . we oppose the depersonalization that reduces human beings to the status of being things." It goes on to say that the deepest human needs cannot be met by better management and improved gadgets. A love for man must overcome the idolatrous worship of things. Right on! They are absolutely right!

Our task is to show them that belief in the dignity and worth of man cannot be sustained on a humanistic basis but is intelligible only in relation to belief in the majesty of God. There is a religious dimension to life which if denied threatens to undermine all other values. Some of the things the counter culture is asking for are right and can best be supplied by a radical Christian faith.

THE AMERICAN WAY OF DEATH

The second lesson the counter culture is teaching us is that the American way of life is frequently a way of death. It has many aspects which are dehumanizing. Why are we raping the earth with industrial technology? Why are we exploring the solar system and not eliminating poverty? Why are we slaughtering Southeast Asians in a senseless war? Are we really prepared to mass murder the Russians or Chinese if they make a wrong move? Why is Calley treated so gently and the Berrigans so callously? Why did we not condemn West Pakistan and help East Pakistan? The kids are nauseated with a system which cannot satisfactorily answer these fundamentally moral questions. And now Nixon tells us to buy more, and save the dollar! Let us by all means remain Number One! The early church did not sit still in the face of social evils. On the strength of divine revelation, they simply refused to worship the emperor and fight his wars. They did not say, "My country, right or wrong," which is basically idolatrous. They had a higher allegiance.

The third lesson springs out of the second. The kids are profoundly turned off by the church because, instead of challenging the status quo, she confirms people in it. The church reminds them of the Republican Party at prayer. It would not be hard to make out a case that the major cause of unbelief today is not that people find the gospel incredible but that they find the churches incredible. They are simply not living by the Word of God.

Often those professing the most faith in that Word are the very last to pay any attention to its ethical demands, and it will come as a complete surprise to them to learn that these secular criticisms of the church are pale indeed beside the divine denunciations about the same things. Ezekiel said in God's name that Israel was a slut. Isaiah said she was dumber than an ox. Jesus called the religious leaders graveyards. God promised to spew out of his mouth churches that did not heed his Word.

The greatest problem today which the kids have pointed out is not the secularism of society but the hypocrisy of the church. It was not always so. The disciples of Jesus were commanded to flesh out the gospel as a radical community acting fearlessly in the light of the eschatological future. It was they who turned the world upside down. They did not go along with material decadence. Poverty was their ideal. Slaves were not slaves to them, but brothers. Indeed those early Christians spoke to Imperial Rome with the same prophetic unreasonableness as the kids are speaking to us. They will not listen to us until they see the apologetics of revolutionary Christianity.

We had better listen to what the Spirit has to say to the churches.

The Thrust of the Counter Culture
by Merold Westphal

We can be grateful to Professor Snyder for not presenting us with another sterile and self-righteous refusal to take the counter culture seriously, a refusal which is usually masked, if possible, by the abstract and pro-forma confession that not everything is perfect and that changes might well be made here and there. In the first place, he is sympathetic to the negations of the counter culture. This is not to say that he takes their slogans as absolute truth, but it is to say that he has both the ability and the disposition to listen; and I suspect in this case that the ability and the disposition are not really different.

At the same time, he recognizes a positive thrust to the counter culture, if not in the form of a program at least in a set of values or attitudes which are affirmed. He also recognizes how deeply counter-cultural the gospel was and is, and that it is universal precisely because it concerns attitudes of the heart and not matters of program.

AFFIRMATIONS AND NEGATIONS
There is, however, an irony about the positive side of the counter culture which deserves more explicit formulation than Snyder gives it. It has to do with certain basic attitudes that are affirmed. America is being called, in biblical language, to repentance and a change of heart. Yet everyone's attention is directed toward what is thoroughly external, the badges which,

as Snyder suggests with good reason, are often the limits of counter-culture radicalism. The counter culture's problem, it seems to me, is not so much the dilemma of finding that its badges either are pre-empted by the Establishment or are proving themselves to be counter-productive, but rather the difficulty of getting beyond the externality of badges when matters of the heart are at issue. It may be just this irony rather than the lack of a program that makes the counter culture look so one-sidedly negative, and it may just be that the Jesus Revolution is the counter culture beginning to overcome this limitation.

Turning to Snyder's interpretation of the counter culture's negations, we find, at first, the attempt to subsume everything under the heading of technology and technocracy. In the economic system, the targets are not only the technology of production but also the technology of distribution (through advertising, marketing research, etc.), as well as the closely related technology of information banks. In the political system, foreign policy is particularly attacked. It may well be that it was Harvard Junior Fellows and not engineers and generals (that is, not the military-industrial complex) which got us into Vietnam, but Snyder detects technological thinking even here when he speaks of treating nations as pawns in a giant game of dominoes, an eloquent if mixed metaphor. Richard Barnett made the same point in *Intervention and Revolution* when he ascribed our post-war foreign policy to the National Security Managers. So to describe the Harvard Junior Fellows and others who have made our foreign policy is to suggest something like the following: The United States, the U.S.S.R. and China are seen as General Motors, Ford and Chrysler, each of which must not only keep its eye on the other two but also on the American Motors of international affairs, the so-called Third World.

THE PERFORMANCE PRINCIPLE
But it is not too helpful to describe what has gone wrong with our economic and political systems as technology run wild, for

it clearly is not simply a matter of machines and automation. This is why Snyder is willing to follow Marcuse in finding technological *thinking* or the *ideology* of technology to be the ultimate target of the counter-culture critique. Marcuse calls it *the performance principle* while Weber long ago labeled it *rationalization*. Whatever the name, the features of this mode of thinking are the same: efficiency and control through calculated action on ideally measurable and, in any case, manipulable variables. It is fundamentally an impersonal approach. Workers, consumers and communists are seen not as persons but as variables which make up production schedules, market research and body counts. It is this view of the world without persons that is being rejected in the complaints of the counter culture about the insensitivity of our society.

It is in these terms that a third major target of the counter culture, largely overlooked by Snyder, needs to be understood; for if there is anything the counter culture is less enthusiastic about than our economic and political systems, it is the family. I shall never forget my own initiation in this regard. It came at the beginning of one of my most exciting experiences as a teacher. My first Kierkegaard seminar was composed of eighteen bright, serious, undergraduate philosophy majors in their junior and senior years. We were reading the second volume of *Either-Or*.

Now I find Judge William's interpretation and defense of marriage there not only conceptually scintillating but thoroughly edifying, at times even lyrical, and I was already gathering momentum in my initial presentation when one of the fellows stopped me and asked who the judge was trying to fool, the reader or himself. Surely his marriage must be in desperate straits, and he probably knows that the young man to whom he is writing is having an affair with his wife; so spirited a sense of marriage gives him away as the gentleman who doth protest too much. I expected a counterresponse but found that not a single member of the seminar besides myself had an exposure to the family which made it possible for him to take Judge William seriously.

My own encounter with the youth culture we are speaking of is largely limited to the academic setting, but if what I perceive there is typical, the rejection of marriage and the family is also to be understood in terms of the performance principle. The family is seen as a place where roles are played and necessary services rendered, rather than as a place where, above all else, persons are together in the mutuality which deserves to be called love. Parents are baby sitters, mothers entertainers, fathers moneymakers.

Rather than trying to develop a discussion of these motifs here, I refer you to the film *Diary of a Mad Housewife*. There one can see in images rather than in concepts what it means for mother and father to be reduced to a network of social and economic functions. Of course, not even sex is invulnerable. As the young writer and the mad housewife get out of bed, he says to her, "Hey, you're good. Who broke you in?" And the chill of those words has not left me—the performance principle in the bedroom. No wonder, as Snyder points out, young people are trying to recover a numinous dimension in sex; nor is it surprising that since they do not perceive the family as giving a more than biological meaning to sex, they often turn to drugs for this purpose.

In summary, I find Snyder's analysis of the counter culture's negations to be sound but in need of extension beyond the economic and political dimensions to the family as well. On the other hand, I am puzzled by his references to a rejection of the normal canons of logic. The long quotation from Roszak strikes me as a very confused discussion of the relationship of mythical to literal thinking, as if these are the only two possibilities, but I do not see what the quotation has to do with logic, nor what it is that leads Snyder to suggest in two places that the counter culture rejects logic.

THE COUNTER CULTURE CONTRA CHRISTIANITY

Finally, I must confess that I find the title of the paper to be misleading. There is so much in it about the counter culture and so little about Christianity. I would like to have seen the counter culture's negations directed not just against the Establishment in general but against the Christian Establishment in particular, or, even more specifically, against the evangelical subculture. For example, it would be fruitful to explore the degree to which the performance principle has become constitutive of our religious life and institutions. We can hardly be said to have escaped the critical eye of the counter culture, and the real test of our willingness to listen is our willingness to see if the shoe fits us, not just if it fits secular, materialistic American culture in general (the latter, of course, always meaning "them").

It is tragic that the critical aspect of the prophetic function comes to us, if at all, so largely through unbelievers. Perhaps if we would open ourselves to hearing the voice of God in what they say (here I want to underscore again Professor Mavrodes's parallel between the counter culture and the Athenian worship of the unknown god; it is precisely in that sense that I want to speak of opening ourselves to hearing the voice of God in what they say), prophets would arise from within the body of Christ who would speak to our own religious establishment as Amos, Jeremiah and Jesus did to theirs.

In addition to seeing the counter culture address the Christian subculture more directly, I would like to have seen the Christian gospel directed against the counter culture more extensively. For example, are not the new values and attitudes of the counter culture (whether or not they are really new) simply another *law* in the Pauline and Lutheran sense? Has the counter culture a gospel to go with its law? Has it a source of freedom to match its aspirations, or is it reduced to impotent hyper-consciousness, like Dostoievsky's underground man? Or, to take another example, how would a response to the performance principle developed from the Christian understanding of *agape* differ from the response Marcuse develops from the notion of *eros*? Agape is a notion of ever-overflowing fullness;

eros is the notion of a striving that stems from emptiness. It seems to me that Sartre has portrayed in a devastating way how the "love" which stems from erotic emptiness can only be the demand to be loved; and when love is nothing but the demand to be loved, there is no love—only the master-slave struggle for domination.

Actually, I'm asking for at least a book, but I would like to have heard more along this line than the comforting assurance that we can pity the shallowness of Consciousness III. I'm afraid this smacks too much, in spite of the author's intentions, of the self-conscious superiority which constantly merges with complacency. So I'm much more enthusiastic about the suggestion which I detect in Snyder's comments that we should learn to pity *ourselves* because we have allowed ourselves both to seem and to be so shallow though possessing what is deepest. Such pity is perhaps the godly fear that produces a repentance that leads to salvation and brings no regrets.

VI
Summaries

The Search for Reality
by Calvin D. Linton

Because the search for reality is inseparable from, if not identical with, the search for personal identity, our papers have had much to say about the "real" self. Such a search is both difficult and painful.

For one thing, the searcher is that which is searched for. The measuring instrument is that which is measured. The sensor is sensed. The one who waits is the one for whom he waits. This presents certain philosophical and psychological problems.

For another thing, it is impossible to look within and not be appalled by what one finds there. Wrote George Meredith in the forty-third sonnet of the *Modern Love* sequence:

> *. . . in tragic life, God wot,*
> *No villain need be! Passions spin the plot;*
> *We are betrayed by what is false within.*

And though Lear's words are directed more specifically at sensuality, they have general applicability: "There's hell, there's darkness, there's the sulphurous pit; burning, scalding, stench, consumption. Fie, fie, fie! pah, pah! Give me an ounce of civit, good apothecary, to sweeten my imagination" (IV, vi, 130 ff).

MAN'S DIVIDED SELF

It may safely be said, I suspect, that over his long history man has expended as much energy and ingenuity in avoiding a knowledge of his real self as in searching honestly for it. And muddling the entire enterprise is the question: Is that part of

myself that is appalled the real me, or is the real me the me that
is appalled by the other me? "There is another man within me
that is angry with me," wrote Sir Thomas Browne. Or, rather
more famously, St. Paul: "For that I do, I allow not; for what I
would, that do I not; but what I hate, that do I" (Rom. 7:15).
"Now then it is no more I that do it, but sin that dwelleth in
me" (Rom. 7:17).

For the modern sophisticate, however, who does not
acknowledge the fact of sin, the reaction to finding something
nasty in the woodshed of his inner self is usually calculated
evasion. Perhaps he divides himself into his "best self" and his
"ordinary self," as Matthew Arnold did, publicly announcing
his allegiance to the former and by word and gesture disavowing
the latter. Or he may accept the nastiness and explain it away in
the light of some convenient psychological, sociological, political or other theory. The resources for doing this are almost
inexhaustible. Perhaps Paul's "sin" becomes "undesirable behavior characteristics," suitable for identification and excision
by some such means as Professor B. F. Skinner advocates. Or
perhaps it is declared to be something like the bound feet of
Chinese women of a former age, distorted by external social
pressures, needing only to be released from all restraint to grow
into the well-shaped and admirable thing it "really" is.

Best of all, perhaps, is simply to sanitize oneself of all nonmaterial, nonquantifiable dimensions, as a biological specimen is
killed and preserved in formaldehyde before being studied.
Everything is left except life. It is inconvenient, of course, that
the real self chiefly manifests its life in moral activity; but
better to have a dead specimen than a dangerous, live one. As
self-named director of research, one is above inquiry oneself,
and, by working hard at "research," can avoid thinking about
oneself at all. This encourages the most elevated kind of hypocrisy, and it has, unhappily, become popular with the young,
who probe the inner nature and motives of all of God's creatures except themselves and wax wondrous indignant at what
they find.

As a minor but typical incident, I recall seeing a young man, dressed and hirsutely adorned in the uniform of the counter culture, drive up and park a Volkswagen bearing a bumper sticker: "Have you said 'Thank you' to a green plant today?" To my own shame, I realized that, actually, I had not. But my chagrin was diminished when I saw him leap out, tramp in the midst of a hedge border and, in order to avoid walking four extra feet to reach the sidewalk, stalk off across the suffering grass. He was probably headed for a rally to "Save the Environment," the site of which would later be identifiable by the piles of trash, the beer cans and the corpses of green plants to whom none had said thank you. Such an episode, however, is probably only an illustration of the rather endearing fatheadedness of the young and is not to be compared, for genuine hypocrisy, with the calculated, double-faced stance of those adults who have had many years within which to develop and polish their schizophrenia. In other words, the problems of infancy are nothing compared to those of adultery.

To their credit, of course, recent generations of young people have sensed the bankruptcy of the philosophy of materialism, technology, machines and statistics—a philosophy lacking vital moral life. However noisily and crudely, they have rejected an education which tells them nothing about themselves and much about metallurgy, social constructs, Middle English philology and the theory of infinite progression.

Unhappily, they have no alternatives to propose. Such counter ideas as they do generally advance are characterized by one feature: they are all *easy*. As Scanzoni points out, they are disinclined to seek their own reality through work, through true vocation, seeing as the announced objective only the "success" of material gain. Many are learning, however, the futility of searching for reality simply by *existing,* living as drones on the efforts of others, insatiably pursuing emotional intensity through rhythm, psychedelic lights and drugs. Such a search is not realistic, either in terms of the God-given, dynamic nature of life, needing to act, to create, to express individuality within order and meaning, nor in terms of the divine judgment after the Fall that by the sweat of his face man should earn his bread.

It is always easy and lazy to be extreme—when angry to shriek, when weary to fall down, when exhausted by the search for the right word to scrawl on the page. But life, like a musical instrument, is a matter of balanced tensions. Trueblood has vividly depicted the need for such harmonious tension between extreme individualism and extreme collectivism in society. "Total concentration on either the self or the community," he writes, "is destructive of human values. The cult of individualism, if consistently applied, would make any genuine civilization impossible. . . . At the same time, the merely collective person is an intrinsic impossibility. . . . They do not become persons at all!"

REASON AND UNREASON

Among the supreme tensions in human existence, out of which comes the deepest harmony of human reality, is that between reason and unreason. The exclusive emphasis on reason can generate the psychological disarray one finds in the young Mill—to launch unruddered on the tossing waves of emotion and impulse quickly brings shipwreck. I have been struck, in reading the papers here presented, by the balance of sensitivity and reasoned logic they exhibit, humane ideas garbed in fitting vocabulary and syntax, energy controlled and guided by reason. These are qualities not much valued by the more audible of the young. The search for reality too often consists of engaging in random talk, in loose, easy emotionalism, as if trying to prove D. H. Lawrence's belief that the reason always misleads us, the feelings never: "Man is a column of blood with a voice, and without the voice he is better."

As Nash points out, anti-intellectualism is a cult symptom. It would, indeed, be difficult to imagine a clearer dissection of the deep-seated irrationality of such writers as Marcuse and Reich than he provides. Among many sentences worth remembering, one is worth engraving: "The message that all in the counter culture should heed is this: if you are sincere in your search for the Real, you must not repudiate the Rational." After all, we are told that Paul "*reasoned* in the synagogue every sabbath," not that he conducted group-gropes there. About those shadow-boxers in the twilight of relativism, Nash says: "You have to watch these relativists. The moment you turn your back, they begin to absolutize."

Such absolutizing, Snyder notes in his analysis of the counter culture, is not done unknowingly or with embarrassment. It is part of the theory, part of the celebration of the "affective state," which all who teach literature remember as a fragment of the jargon of the "New Critics" of the thirties. We remember that these critics scorned all facts about a poem, all rational efforts to understand it in terms of its time, its author's biography or its frame of reference. Instead, its reality was sought exclusively in the effect the work of art has on the individual's sensibility. Granted the need to see literary art *as* literature, not merely historical and autobiographically revealing documents, the tendency was to deny rational relevance to anything but itself. A poem is about itself. So life is entirely inturned, about itself, dissociated from all else, as so gruesomely taught by the Dadaists.

Instant service from all the tools of technology; impassioned attack on their existence. This is one of the contradictions of the counter culture. This and other mysteries are probed clinically but humanely from the psychiatrist's point of view by Nicholi. Nor does he permit us the luxury of protective distance from the problems. Human differences, he notes, are less significant than human similarities, and we study diseases we ourselves are subject to. Rebellion, violence, impassioned judgment—this is tasty food to the beast in all of us. In some dark recess of our fallen nature we all understand, and in some measure respond to, Satan's magnificent (and totally irrational) speeches in *Paradise Lost*. As Mark Twain said, human nature is very widely distributed among people.

But I must not, by narrowly selective emphasis, distort the

admirably broad and comprehensive points of view encom-
passed in these papers. Above all, I must not speak as if youth
were the target, as if youth were folly, age wisdom. Confusion
about personal identity is not a new problem. It began when
Adam denounced his true allegiance and identity, sought
another ("ye shall be as gods") and, like the dog in the fable,
dropped the reality he had for the reflection in the pool. In the
shorter view, surely the identity and reality crisis has been epi-
demic in the Western world since the Romantic Revolution, the
great turn inward. A generation now elderly or dead recognized
itself fifty years ago in Eliot's "The Hollow Men":

> This is the dead land
> This is the cactus land
> Here the stone images
> Are raised, here they receive
> The supplication of a dead man's hand
> Under the twinkle of a fading star.

Indeed, none of our papers permits us to stand as the Director of Research, examining other people. We have seen ourselves
as well. Our youth have inherited a world of distorted values
and misshapen purposes, and we have long known it. For some
in this room, the sudden coming over to "our side" in some
matters by youthful activists has been both heartening and dis-
maying. This is peculiarly apparent with the "Jesus people," but
perceptibly so as well in lesser issues. I remember, for example,
certain feeble words I uttered and wrote back in the fifties
about the materialization and dehumanization of man through
scientism and social statistics, and I hear their echoes now at
student protest gatherings. All of us who teach the humanities
warned against vastly increasing power without increasing wisdom. In those days, such views were felt to be mildly annoying,
perhaps, and obviously wrong-headed. Anyone with any brains
at all in 1955 knew that man's progress (and the "fact" of
progress was never questioned) depended on better technology,
not better people.

But it was in 1956 that Samuel Beckett wrote hauntingly of

the erosion of personal identity. After completing his novel *The Unnamable,* he said: "The French work [he wrote the original novel in French, of course] brought me to the point where I felt I was saying the same thing over and over again. For some authors writing gets easier the more they write. For me it gets more and more difficult. For the area of possibilities gets smaller and smaller. . . . At the end of my work there is nothing but dust. . . . In the last book [*The Unnamable*] there is complete disintegration. No 'I,' no 'being.' No nominative, no accusative, no verb. There is no way to go on."

Those colleges and universities which, abdicating their role as moral guides, squeezed out everything of a spiritual nature and taught nothing but quantities and physical relationships were wastelands, deserts. Idealistic young people, dying of thirst, found no flowing streams, no wells, no fountains. Literary art seemed determined to plumb the depths but never to scale the heights. As a kind of composite book review of modern novels, *Punch* a few years ago printed a "review" of a book called *My Sewer, My Bride* "by Ned Rutt, Calder & Boyers, 25 shillings. The story concerns the tribulations of a teen-age Riviera ponce who is struck on the head during a mescaline orgy aboard the private jetliner of ace pusher Erskine Marowitz. The boy, Alice Kraus, subsequently loses his memory, and, wandering in North Africa as a dime-a-dance hostess, finally finds true happiness through suicide."

Never doubting that youth would eagerly embrace the materialistic values of their generation, adult college faculties and administrators were dismayed when they rebelled. As Kingman Brewster of Yale said in 1970, thousands of young people were in college without knowing why they were there and actively wishing they were somewhere else. This was one of the causes of the generation gap. To many of the older generation, who remember times of financial depression when the possession of a college degree made the difference between having a job and food or having neither, the benefit of going to college was perfectly clear. To many of the younger generation, who took affluence for granted, this attitude was condemned as mere commercialism. Many of them, on the contrary, shouted that one goes to college in order to participate in society and to change it.

A LIBERAL EDUCATION

Actually, of course, neither purpose is now, or ever has been, the chief reason why that difficult-to-define thing called a "liberal education" came into existence. If one's purpose is solely to gain information and skills which he can sell at a profit for the rest of his life, he should go to a vocational school—a perfectly worthy and honorable purpose. If one's purpose is to change society, why take the detour through college? If one already knows exactly what is wrong with society—and all young people are sure they do—why not get at curing it right away?

The real purpose of a liberal education is so difficult, so burdensome, so wearying and so important that we quite understandably hate to face up to it. Its purpose is quite simple: to gain wisdom. And central to wisdom is the search for reality. Wisdom is quite different from information and skills, and quite different from social action. The opposite of wisdom is not ignorance or social inaction; it is folly. Many intelligent and highly educated people are foolish; many unlearned people are wise. Many social activists are foolish, and many who lead lives of quiet influence are wise. There is no equation.

How hard it is for all of us, regardless of age, to learn that wisdom begins with self-knowledge. How much easier and how much more fun it is to judge others than to judge ourselves. One of the most comforting and pleasing thoughts in the world is to believe that the world's problems are all caused by other people and that we ourselves have somehow escaped the universal infection. The sacred text relating to this folly begins rather roughly: "Thou hypocrite!"

If we wish to see the cause of the world's misery, we should not look into the face of our brother but into the mirror. There we shall see all the selfishness, greed, cruelty and self-righteousness that plague our world. But look deep and perhaps we can see something of the wonder and glory God originally planted there—something so wonderful he sent his Son to redeem it, though he went through death and hell to do it. What he saved is what is real about us. Scanzoni points out that self-esteem is often the result of measuring the esteem in which we are held by others. Behold, then, God's esteem for us!

It is apparent that any sense of reality must emanate from a knowledge of that which determines reality. Anything less is simply a statement of what I myself *think* reality is. In my own view, the inability of the "natural man" to determine his real self is owing to his lack of one-third of his being, by reason of the Fall. That is, he retains his body and his soul (both sadly marred), but his spirit is dead in trespasses and sins, unless made alive by the power of God in redemption. Nor can this missing spiritual dimension be considered as leaving man with "two-thirds of his identity," for the spirit is the key to all the rest, the channel of knowledge of God, from whom alone may one learn what is real. Only God is absolute reality. All else is his creation, a manifestation of his will. As creatures made in his image and for his glory, we discover our own reality not by looking inward, to self, but outward, to him. Our thoughts follow reality only in his footsteps.

What Is Man on Earth For?
by Carl F. H. Henry

The counter-cultural protest is multi-pronged, as our essayists have been reminding us, and many of these prongs have pricked us during our discussion of the modern search for reality. The fundamental question that rises to the surface of the culture controversy again and again is: What is man on earth *for*?

The indictments of scientism and technocratic civilization, of materialistic affluence, and of the contemporary lust for dollars and things, imply an answer to this question. The alienated young indict the modern scientific world view insofar as it reduces external reality to predictable sequences of impersonal events and thereby eclipses the significance of personal acts, purpose and decision; omnipresent technology they deplore for its ongoing erosion of human values. The priority of the material they scorn in their detachment from social affluence and also by their disinterest in the prevalent commitment to daily work as basically a means to private wealth or executive prestige in the world of business. Their revolt carries over into spirited indictments of the mass media, now often depicted as the mirror of the American military establishment or as the propagandist of Euro-American, white pseudovalues, values that while offering new selfhood actually advance the commercial exploitation of mankind.

THE ROLE OF CHRISTIANITY
Amid this ferment, one senses an increasing disposition of social

critics to blame all the ugly modern alternatives on Christianity. If one is mindful of two factors, it becomes apparent why the Christian religion should so frequently surface into the discussion. First, historic Christianity did indeed contribute decisively to the development of natural science, to the emergence of a distinctive work ethic and to the world-wide propagandizing of a message of new life and values. Second, modern Christianity, which has often diluted its biblical heritage, has not infrequently, through compromise and concession, blurred the distinction between technological exploitation of the earth and man's moral dominion over it, between work as a stewardship and service and work as a means of material aggrandizement, between the world-wide extension of the gospel and the transmission of Western culture-motifs.

Amid the truly legitimate elements in the counter-cultural complaint, the greatest service that Christian intellectuals can provide is to discriminate what is worthy from what is unworthy in the present social ferment and to reinforce what is right. In the course of Western history, the Christian church as an institution has often made a costly identification with one or another cultural manifestation; it would be the costliest mistake of all were she now simply to champion the status quo.

Present indications are that the youth revolt does not sufficiently pervade prevailing culture patterns to assure any fundamental change. The pressure of job-material survival-needs holds down the number of those who through hard drug addiction defect to Cloud Seven, and those not born to affluence are striving for the very material advantages which culture-alienated whites renounce. Leaders of the revolutionary thrust, moreover, are limited in number; the same radical activists must maintain high mobility and visibility to give the impression of wide support and enthusiasm for social revolution.

Yet the most important concern before the Christian community is not the statistical probability of success or nonsuccess of the youth revolt. Taken on its own premises, Christianity has from the beginning been in its own way counter-cultural. Professor Snyder therefore scores the point well that "Christians are a counter culture of longer pedigree than beat, Bohemian or hip." If culture is defined as the collective achievement of human ingenuity, then Christianity in the light of divine revelation and demand must judge the whole of it adversely, for Christianity illumines all culture, subculture and counter culture—including even what passes for Christian culture—by the Word of God. While we are, as Snyder reminds us, to "salt the earth of technitronic machinery and counter culture alike," Christianity at the same time proclaims the one enduring society to be the Kingdom of God, ideally anticipated in the church's life in the world. Christianity is pro-Kingdom rather than merely anticultural; not for nothing did Jesus orient his disciples to pray, "Thy kingdom come."

PERSONAL VALUES

If we inquire about the positive distinctives of the present counter-cultural revolt, we are told to observe its emphasis on personal values, a fundamental priority that technocratic scientism and secular materialism seem to obscure. These values are identified mainly as macro-ethical concerns—problems of international war, global pollution, racial bias. The churches, it is often complained, concentrate instead on micro-ethics. Nothing should diminish the importance of youth's questioning of the easy acceptance of modern warfare and of the easy rejection of those who stand outside our own circle of privilege and pigment. Yet one criticism to be made of this dichotomy of macro-ethics and micro-ethics, although it is hardly the deepest criticism to be made of the counter-cultural stance, is that vices like covetousness, theft, adultery, lies, and so on, are not as unsymptomatic of a sick society as fledgling philosophers and professional politicians often imply in their disdain for a Puritan ethic. Just social structures cannot long endure without men of good will. Love for neighbor is still an important umbrella commandment that panoplies duties to others.

I am not suggesting that counter-cultural youth is disinterested in interpersonal love; the ready acceptance of others, irrespective of creed or color, is one of its hallmarks. Yet what it values as interpersonal love ignores much in the way of love for neighbor that the second great commandment implies, as for example when disaffiliated youth coordinate political concern with sexual lassitude. The alienated young laugh at women who strive to outdress each other but lack scruples about the underdressing and undressing of teenagers. Much of youth's personal ethics is now a whirlwind churning with religious rebelliousness and seeking to outstrip a fatigued conscience. If Pascal thought life's odds are such that man should wager on the reality of God, contemporary youth seem willing to chance it with the modern theologians that there is no hell.

THE DEEPER WEAKNESS

Yet the deeper weakness of the counter-cultural championing of personal values lies in its virtual godlessness. While the duty of man is love of neighbor, his first duty is love of God. The theological vagrancy of the counter culture reinforces an astute observation made by Dr. W. Harry Jellema to directors of the Institute for Advanced Christian Studies, namely, that its characteristics are to be located more in what it lacks than in what it professes. For more than a generation the American classroom from elementary learning onwards has been out of touch with the unique spiritual and moral heritage of Judeo-Christian realities; this detachment from God, transcendent revelation and fixed morality and truth now abandons the religious life of contemporary man into chaos. The present generation suffers from more than spiritual memory-loss; it has been denied an understanding of the most influential religious heritage in human history. Adrift outside the orbit of biblical realities, it whirls on without fixed ethical controls and without any sure sense of direction and destiny.

There is, as we know, a vigorous mystical thrust in the counter-cultural quest for a new consciousness. Whether they resort to hallucinatory drugs or to religious phenomena, alienated young people are deliberately scrambling over the confining walls of scientific method to find hopeful ways of access to a transcendent reality. Personal values tend to gain whatever transcendent status they have within the nebulous mists of spiritual mysticism.

Professor Nash exposes a devastating weakness in this counter-cultural thrust, one that runs through its literature no less than its life style, that is, the absence of any rational methodology by which to check the validity of any of its claims or conclusions. Scholars who rely on the sword of epistemic relativity to disgorge the views of others have no reason to expect anyone to defer to their own pontifications about the nature and drift of reality as the last word. The flight from reason and from the canons of logic offers no secure haven whatever; it is a veritable flight from reality. Nash is therefore on solid ground in his warning to the counter culture: "If you are sincere in your search for the Real, you must not repudiate the Rational." A generation in trouble may do without a great deal, but if it tries to get along without reason it will forfeit any and every reason for living. The question What is man on earth *for*? cannot be isolated from the question What *reason* is there, if any, for my being on earth?

Christian theism focuses on the reality of a rational Creator who establishes and undergirds the cosmic significance of reason and logic. Christianity, therefore, points to a transcendent reality that requires and reinforces rather than relinquishes the highest use of reason. The Christian doctrine of revelation calls not for the crucifixion of reason but rather for the crucifixion of the rebellious nature of man. It regards not human speculation but the Living God as the source of truth. It insists nonetheless on the logicality of faith and invites human reason to test its truth-claims by logical criteria.

Professor Linton has ably scored the point that reality—even our own reality—is not to be discovered by merely looking inward to self. It is to be discovered, rather, by looking to God, for man is by creation made in his Maker's image for God's glory, and "our thoughts follow reality only in His footsteps." For the Christian, therefore, reality leads at once to the Living God as the self-revealed, intelligible Creator, whose moral law inescapably brackets and judges even the befogged renegades who beat against his directives.

The counter culture's dismissal of technocratic scientism as the addictive mythology of modern Western man is as cutting as it is cunning. But insofar as youth's revolt against technocratic impersonalism grounds its alternative in irrational mystic experience, the counter culture simply substitutes one mythology for another. The best anchorages for any recovery of personal values in modern life are still the revelation of the Living God and the doctrinal logic of the Christian perspective.

THE JESUS FREAKS

What then, it may be asked, about the Jesus freaks, whose plunge to a spiritual alternative has the merit, at least, of a return to God and his authoritative Word, and embraces a vital personal relationship to King Jesus? Their open identification with the God of the Bible and their bold "One Way" witness "in Jesus' name" stamped them from the outset as apostolically venturesome for the gospel. At the same time, their existential orientation and shallow doctrinal logic left them vulnerable to extreme charismatic claims and to fanatical excesses. Their plea for an uncomplicated Christianity involved more complications than they could foresee. Returning to the Acts of the Apostles, they sought for themselves an extension of apostolic gifts and miracles. The lasting nature of this movement was therefore in doubt, and its final character remains still to be clarified. There are bright signs, however, that the Jesus-freak mood is yielding in many places to a Jesus-follower commitment; in ever larger numbers these young Christians are seeking a biblical understanding of the experience they have had. The world can at least identify these professing Christians by their radiance, a characteristic that they are determined to match with a spontaneous love. They consider God's promises able to pierce the shades of adolescent darkness and confidently expect the grim shackles of their night of sin to yield to Christ's releasing power. They openly pity those who hope to buck the whole gamut of teen-age temptation without God and who while lacking new life in Christ mistakenly think they have plumbed all the exhilarating experiences young life has to offer.

It is true, of course, that many of the Jesus followers have deep questions about the institutional church and about the role of the clergy as traditionally conceived; many consider three years of seminary training to be a waste of time. Such reservations cannot be met by simply defending the established patterns of education or of clericalism. The questions young people are asking require far more than this. While growing numbers of Jesus followers are shunning the pulpit ministry as a vocation, they are eager nonetheless to master the logic of Christian belief and to wrestle the issues of theology and apologetics. Their generation has, in fact, much to say to the Christian community that they find so hard to understand; the failure in intelligible communication is not necessarily only theirs. Not long ago a Canadian audience of young Jesus followers burst into laughter at the close of a so-called Christian film. Later when the stunned sponsors of the film asked what had been so funny, a spokesman for the young people answered: "Well, in the closing minutes the guy in the film got saved for absolutely no reason whatever." In this symbolic reaching for a rationale, we, too, join those who ask what man is on the earth *for,* and seek a hope unblemished by hallucination and radiant with reason.

Participants

Participants in an invitational conference sponsored by the Institute for Advanced Christian Studies in Chicago in October, 1971: "Christian Perspective on THE SEARCH FOR REALITY in Modern Life"

V. Elving Anderson, Ph.D., Professor of Genetics and Cell Biology, and Assistant Director, Dight Institute of Human Genetics, University of Minnesota.

David Carley, M.A., Ph.D., President of Inland Steel Development Co., and Regent, University of Wisconsin.

James Daane, A.B., B.D., Th.D., Director of Doctorate of Ministry, Fuller Theological Seminary.

Douglas D. Feaver, B.A., M.A., Ph.D., Professor of Classics, Lehigh University, and Director, Humanities Perspective on Technology.

Carl F. H. Henry, Ph.D., Editor at Large, *Christianity Today,* and Professor at Large, Eastern Baptist Theological Seminary.

Arthur F. Holmes, A.B., M.A., Ph.D., Professor of Philosophy, Wheaton College.

James M. Houston, M.A., B.Sc., D.Phil., Principal of Regent College, and Lecturer in Geography, University of British Columbia.

Calvin D. Linton, A.B., M.A., Ph.D., Dean of the College of Arts and Sciences, George Washington University.

George I. Mavrodes, B.S., B.D., M.A., Ph.D., Associate Professor of Philosophy, University of Michigan.

David O. Moberg, A.A., A.B., M.A., Ph.D., Professor of Sociology, and Chairman, Department of Sociology and Anthropology, Marquette University.

Ronald H. Nash, A.B., M.A., Ph.D., Professor of Philosophy, and Head, Department of Philosophy and Religion, Western Kentucky University.

Armand M. Nicholi II, B.A., M.D., Faculty of Harvard Medical School, Harvard University, and private practice, Cambridge.

Clark H. Pinnock, A.B., Ph.D., Professor of Theology, Trinity Evangelical Divinity School.

John H. Scanzoni, A.B., Ph.D., Professor of Sociology, Indiana University.

John W. Snyder, A.B., B.D., M.A., Ph.D., Executive Vice Chancellor, University of California at Santa Barbara.

D. Elton Trueblood, A.B., S.T.B., Ph.D., Professor at Large, Earlham College, Richmond, Indiana.

Merold Westphal, B.A., M.A., Ph.D., Associate Professor of Philosophy, Yale University.